The Paradox of Skills

STUDIES IN INCLUSIVE EDUCATION
Volume 11

Scope
This series addresses the many different forms of exclusion that occur in schooling across a range of international contexts and considers strategies for increasing the inclusion and success of all students. In many school jurisdictions the most reliable predictors of educational failure include poverty, Aboriginality and disability. Traditionally schools have not been pressed to deal with exclusion and failure. Failing students were blamed for their lack of attainment and were either placed in segregated educational settings or encouraged to leave and enter the unskilled labour market. The crisis in the labour market and the call by parents for the inclusion of their children in their neighbourhood school has made visible the failure of schools to include all children.

Drawing from a range of researchers and educators from around the world, Studies in Inclusive Education will demonstrate the ways in which schools contribute to the failure of different student identities on the basis of gender, race, language, sexuality, disability, socio-economic status and geographic isolation. This series differs from existing work in inclusive education by expanding the focus from a narrow consideration of what has been traditionally referred to as special educational needs to understand school failure and exclusion in all its forms. Moreover, the series will consider exclusion and inclusion across all sectors of education: early years, elementary and secondary schooling, and higher education.

The Paradox of Skills

*Widening Participation, Academic Literacy
& Students' Skills Centres*

Linda Anne Barkas
Teesside University, UK

SENSE PUBLISHERS
ROTTERDAM/BOSTON/TAIPEI

A C.I.P. record for this book is available from the Library of Congress.

ISBN: 978-94-6091-398-3 (paperback)
ISBN: 978-94-6091-399-0 (hardback)
ISBN: 978-94-6091-400-3 (e-book)

Published by: Sense Publishers,
P.O. Box 21858,
3001 AW Rotterdam,
The Netherlands
www.sensepublishers.com

Printed on acid-free paper

DEDICATION

In memory of my Father Edward John Bruce

TABLE OF CONTENTS

ACKNOWLEDGEMENTS

I should like to thank Professor Lorna Unwin, for her guidance and patience during the supervision of my thesis, from which the evidence for the book is drawn. I also extend my gratitude to Dr. Anne-Marie Bathmaker and Professor Roger Slee for their interest in my work. I am particularly grateful to Professor Slee and Michel Lokhorst for providing the opportunity to put the story of the SSC into print. I am grateful for the friendship of Geraldine Richmond and Suzanne Heywood, and thank them both for our wonderful conversations on the changing nature of higher education. I am also most appreciative of their help with the proof reading of the final version of the manuscript. I should also like to thank Chris Barkas for his forbearance, and his efforts to care for and entertain all our animals while I worked on the manuscript.

I have checked the text and references several times. I can only apologise if there are any errors I have overlooked.

INTRODUCTION

There are two things you should remember when dealing with parallel universes. One, they're not really parallel, and two; they're not really universes (Adams, quoted in Chown, 2007, 3).

INTRODUCTION

Physicists and cosmologists have long debated the complexity of the known and the unknown aspects of the universe but in 2010, they are no closer to a definitive answer on the origins of the cosmos. They are however, respectful of different theories even if they do not share the same views (Halsey, 1992). This courtesy, however, is not extended to the post-16 education sector, where one particular viewpoint, even if there is little, if any supporting evidence, appears to dominate. Unwin (2004b) uses the term a 'parallel universe' to explain how the prejudice to other areas of study has manifested in the thinking and attitudes of policy developments in relation to vocational, as against academic education. The issue of whether or not 'skills' exist in general contexts, surrounds both vocational and academic education, so I should like to refer again to Unwin's (2004b) term and develop this use of an analytical metaphor still further, and argue that in terms of different values, there are 'multi-verses' existing in higher education.

The discourse of skills is vastly complicated (see inter alia, Ainley 2000; Hyland, 2003; Unwin, 2009) so I shall focus my argument by examining how definitions of skills and teaching manifest in the discourse surrounding three of these multi-verses, namely the role of higher education; widening participation and students' skills centres. Each of these universes is made up of 'worlds' whereby the dominant ideas prevail in that particular world, without any consideration of opposing views that exist simultaneously. So the different views may as well, as Unwin (2004b) has shown, be in a parallel universe thus creating conflict and tension in universities, described by Winter (2009) as different schisms because managers and academics often have values that are incongruent to each other (Winter, 2009, 122).

The term *multi-verse* can symbolically capture the nature of the contradictory and conflicting language that exists in current thinking about the role and function of universities in modern society. Within each of these universes, there exist a number of different dimensions within 'worlds of thought' whereby the supporters of a viewpoint appear to genuinely believe their view is the only 'true reality'. They choose to appear, or their actions seem to suggest, they are oblivious to the existence of the thought forms that exist in any other dimension within their world. A viewpoint seems to dominate a line of action, as its supporters claim that their view is how 'their universe' exists; thereby dismissing as irrelevant the idea that there could, in fact, be other 'universes' with entirely different thoughts to their perceived viewpoint (Ainley, 2000; Hyland, 2004; Kenny, 2009; Young and Muller 2010). The use of an analytical metaphor provides a mechanism to explore these diverse viewpoints to show how they impact, creating serious problems in the system, resulting in unintentional, impossible situations for academic staff working in SSCs.

The dimensional thoughts within worlds circulate around different 'suns' of core beliefs and so when debates take place about what role SSCs have in higher education, the empirical ideas underlying any given argument have fundamentally different starting points and definitions, so intention and meaning, becomes both 'lost in translation and lost in transmission' (Gee, 2000; Lum, 2004). As with any navigational system, whether they are on land, water, air or in outer-space, it is important to have a point of orientation, so for the purpose of organisation, the focal point in this book is academic literacy. Although the SSC was set up from within a 'skills agenda', students' queries at the SSC were not about study or employability skills, but were connected to how to write about the knowledge of a given subject, and this is termed 'academic literacy' (Hyland, 2004).

At the time of writing this book, the world was in the midst of a global economic recession. In early 2010, massive cuts to public services had been announced by the government. This was to mean the higher education budgets were to be decreased by at least 9% (Newman, 2010). Yet it was an entirely different story just over ten years ago. The National Inquiry into Higher Education, the Dearing Report, (1997) was the first major review of higher education since the Robbins Report of 1963. The Dearing Report (1997) emphasised the requirement for universities to provide more opportunities to widen participation in higher education. This Report was the first of many policies that government introduced to reshape the nature of higher education provision in England.

The book is aimed at researchers investigating the background to widening participation as it has developed over the past few decades. It may also be of interest to researchers examining the changing attitudes to learning and teaching in higher education. The purpose of the book is to highlight some 'snapshots in time' to show how key aspects of higher education policies and the related discourse impacted on the attitudes to students' learning in higher education. In response to these government policies, universities introduced many strategies to restructure and reorganise their educational courses. This book draws on a longitudinal study into one such measure, a centralised study skills centre, (SSC) to explore how the differentiated discourse surrounding the policies imposed to bring about changes to the higher education are both paradoxical and contradictory, resulting in disjointed and fragmented views of what is meant by an institution of 'higher learning'.

SSCs were widely adopted in post-1992 universities across the higher education sector, but not as much in the older, pre-1992 universities (Thomas, Quinn, Slack and Casey 2003). Wingate (2007) conducted a random search of the internet of 10 pre-1992 and 10 post-1992 universities and all but two of them offered some form of study support. This method of meeting students' learning needs is known as a 'bolt-on' approach (Bennett, Dunne and Carre, 2000) as against lecturers providing 'an embedded' process of guidance and instruction on how to learn and write about knowledge within the structure of a subject (Lea and Stierer, 2000). By exploring how and why, the 'bolt-on' approach (Bennet et al., 2000) took such a hold in higher education; it is possible to see the strengthening of normalisation of beliefs through what Bernstein (2000) called the rise of genericism.

The 'snapshots in time' have been chosen because they explain how contradictory issues in learning and teaching were exposed through a 'grounded theory' (Glaser and Strauss 1967) application during the research into the SSC. Different views of what is meant by 'skills' and their application to learning were revealed through the study of the work of SSCs, that can be seen to reflect on a micro-scale, the larger challenges faced by universities. The challenges originate from four broad aspects of higher education. Firstly, how well universities have responded to governments demands to widen access, primarily over the past decade, and secondly, in the same time period, how the 'business language and idea' of higher education as a product to market, has replaced the value of 'knowledge' (Young, 2009).

The difficulties, however, in how universities actually 'deliver this higher education product' are either ignored or dismissed, and these issues are therefore, demonstrated in practical terms, in the third and fourth aspects of higher education. Thirdly, to serve the learning needs of all the extra students, universities have failed to sufficiently engage in working out what and how it was going to provide the extra help. Fourthly, in the rush for expansion of numbers, the needs of staff and the related disciplinary differences between subjects was totally overlooked. Superimposed on these four broad aspects are five complex dimensions: academic literacy, skills, knowledge, business and technology and teaching, that influence the four aspects through: the policy discourse, the changing role of universities, human and social capital theories, lifelong learning and access (See Table 4 in Chapter 2).

These competing ideologies of influence have therefore, resulted in paradoxes and ironies in higher education on a massive scale. There is extensive literature on each of these ideological aspects (See inter alia Ainley, 2000; Barnett, 1998; Bathmaker, 2007; Scott, 1998; Slee, 2001;), so the purpose in this book is to provide an introduction to some of them by explaining how the issues were 'grounded' (Glaser and Strauss, 1967) in the work of the SSC and how they were discovered over the decade of the longitudinal study. As the issues are vast and wide ranging, I have chosen to draw on the empirical evidence of the research to explore how the specific nature of the two main areas of conflict are inexplicably woven into all the other aspects of thinking about what it means to provided a 'higher education'. These two main areas of conflict are 'teaching' and 'skills'. I shall argue that the two main areas of conflict arise from disagreements surrounding the role of higher education in society; policies for widening participation and the introduction of centralised students' skills centres.

I shall draw on the research into an SSC to explain how these viewpoints caused problems for the staff working in the researched institution. Although in the past decade, many universities, have embraced different approaches to widening participation either by reviewing their minimum entry qualifications, and/or introducing subject specific, accredited writing modules (Preece and Godfrey, 2009; Wingate, 2007), at the time of the formal research, many universities still offered generic, study and writing services through centralised services (Thomas et al., 2003).

Perhaps the greatest irony of successful widening participation strategies in universities is the fact that SSCs still exist at all in 2010. In some institutions SSCs were set up in a desperate attempt to provide a unit that could provide 'help' to this ever increasing number of students, but no regard was given beforehand to deciding exactly what could possibly be offered in terms of 'help'. Concepts, definitions, boundaries and policies were not even conceived, let alone thought through. If they had been, the impossibility of such a service would have been identified. On the one hand, students, subject teaching staff and management, generally welcomed the efforts made by the staff in the SSC, but on the other, they do not want to admit they actually needed the SSCs, or even worse, that the SSC could not provide the 'help', so chose to distance themselves from the issues that the SSC presented, shielding themselves behind the mistaken belief that SSC could provide none-contextualised 'skills'. In this belief system, the academic tutor and coordinator of the SSC, in turn, is 'demoted' and becomes a *persona non grata,* a sort of humanoid, *partial academic,* not a *proper lecturer* but a *skills tutor,* a *minister without a portfolio.* As I write in 2010, I am still involved in a University and College Union challenge over what the institution's personnel department means by its use of the term 'skills' on the role description for the work in the SSC.

The resulting implications of the different perceptions of the issues involved in 'higher skills' writing and study skills, manifests in a distorted and confused dis-course; which has serious consequences for academic staff who help develop students' learning in any way either by working in the centre and teaching or researching students' needs.

Even when evidence was provided to prove that students had complex, learning and writing needs, the managers of the researched institution, refused to accept the study's findings (Barkas, 2008). This was to have a long term, negative impact on the staff who worked in the SSC. A further irony is that while the students could accept the reality of the situation in SSCs, the personnel department, some academic staff and the managers, could not. The possible reason behind their denial or refusal to accept the reality of students' needs and the different viewpoints are therefore, explored by encapsulating the nature of the views within worlds, in the different universes, and of what is perceived as a *higher education.*

I will discuss the dimensions of each of these concepts in the next chapter where I will also revisit the nature of the language and discourse of skills. The following section, however, will now outline the background in terms of policy development that led to the belief that SSCs could be the answer to students' needs.

Background

The belief that more graduates in the workforce will increase the prosperity of nations has become a core educational policy over the past few decades, particularly in western democracies (Brown et al., 2008). In England, widening participation in universities has become the focus of the government's education policy since the 1963 Robbins Report, but it has gained significant momentum in the past 20 or so years through, in particular, the 1992 Further and Higher Education Act, the Kennedy and Dearing Reports of 1997 and the 2003 White Paper, The Future of

Higher Education, and the 2004 Higher Education Act.[1] In its National Learning Targets of 1999, the Labour government set a target for 50% of all 18–30 year olds to participate in higher education by the year 2010. This was linked to policies designed to ensure a qualified workforce in the UK population as part of a national skills strategy. The participation target also included a directive to encourage young people from families who had not previously experienced post-compulsory education to enter higher education (HEFCE, 2001). Hence, the target was seen to be aimed at both competitiveness and a social inclusion agenda.

To ensure an increasing number of people obtain graduate qualifications, has resulted in an increasing marketisation of higher education as a consumerist product. This has changed the emphasis on the value of a higher education from its fundamental intrinsic value, which could be translated to a positive influence for a society's development (see inter alia Barnett, 1994; Young 2006; Young and Muller, 2010). The government's view that universities exist only to serve the economy was emphasised in physical terms when the name of the Department of Education and Skills was changed in 2007 to the Department for Innovation, Universities and Skills (DIUS), then merged in June 2009 (Parry, 2009) into another structure, the Department for Business, Innovation and Skills (BIS 2009).

Mills (2007) has argued that the belief that universities can prepare graduates as an 'economic product' of value in the job market, is flawed. This is because one theoretical model has been superimposed on another. Mills (ibid, 15) has said that, "the real problem lies in the way this 'student as consumer model' has been conflated with an older model: 'business as customer'. The two models are incompatible". In 2010, the world was undergoing a global economic recession. Past trends have shown that, generally, when employment prospects are poor, universities have seen a rise in applications (Coffield, 2000). Although the links to economic success from the successful completion of degree level studies is still unclear in 2009, the pressure on Higher Education Institutions (HEIs) to admit and retain more students remains.

The view that more highly skilled workers would increase prosperity was practically demonstrated by the government's introduction in 2001 of the Learning and Skills Council (LSC) in England with a brief to "plan, fund, target and inspect" the existing and emerging vocational provision, and to oversee the coordination of what has been termed the 'learning and skills sector' (Steer, Edward, Hodgson and Coffield, 2005, 1). The government's emphasis on skill development that commenced with the *Dearing Report* (1997) was consolidated in the Learning and Skills Act 2000 which brought together the providers of post-16 education under the direction of the Learning Skills Council; a department that in 2009 was then to be divided in two in 2010 (Parry, 2009). This was followed by the government commissioned Leitch review of Skills in 2006, a report that was heavily criticised for its lack of specificity (Unwin, 2009). These policy developments created challenges for post-compulsory education and training in relation to how they coped with increasing student numbers. The challenges arise from the need to meet the government's target in three fundamental areas. Firstly, all institutions must present clear admissions policies. Secondly, they must offer appropriate courses and thirdly, they must retain the students they admit. These issues are connected so they are often interlinked in returns to post-compulsory and higher education but different trends emerge (National Audit Office, 2006).

In 2007, 411, 971 students were registered to start a course in a higher education institution in the autumn of that year showing a 5.8% rise from 2006. (HESA, 2007). As more students have decided to apply to university, the pressure to obtain good grades in their General Certificate in Education at Advanced levels (GCE A levels) has also increased. Although a number of different vocational and academic qualifications are awarded points within the UCAS system, the GCE A-level and equivalent qualifications remain the most common entry qualifications for entrants to a higher education. The GCE A level qualification has been the main entry qualification for universities for over fifty years but in order to meet government's target for increased participation in a university education, some universities or higher education institutions (HEIs) (*higher education institution* is the term that has been introduced to describe an institution or college that that offers higher education courses) reviewed their minimum entrance qualifications and/ or adjusted their tariff score (UCAS, 2005). The tariff score accords a numeric value to different types and levels of eligible qualifications to provide universities with a report of students' academic achievement (HESA, 2007). Universities and HEIs set a tariff requirement for entry into their degree courses of study. Points are accorded to different subjects. For example, if a student passed 3 General Certificates of Education at Advanced Levels (GCE A-levels) at an 'A' grade, this would mean a point score of 360 (UCAS, 2005). Over the past decade however, the post-1992 universities in particular, have not become homogeneous institutions, with much diversity of practise developing. For example, in response to addressing retention issues, although many institutions lowered their minimum standards to admit more students in the late 1990s, many universities have now reviewed or increased their minimum entry standards (Lucas 2004; Parry, Davies and Williams 2004; Thomas, Quinn, Slack and Casey 2003).

As more students obtain good GCE A-level grades, as soon as the results are known there is a continued revival every year in the media of the debate as to whether or not GCE A-levels have become easier or less suitable for entry into a modern degree course. An illustration of this may be shown by an academic tutor who expressed their view in a comment in the Times Higher Education Supplement, that students language skills were declining; "what worries me is the kind of situation I have encountered recently at university where the English of some graduates is so poor that they cannot grasp whether the lecturer is affirming a proposition or denying it" (Harris, 2007, 15). The decline in language ability was also shown by statistics produced by the then Department for Education and Skills (DfES) in 2006 showed that 300,000 pupils (47%) had left school at 16 years of age without attaining level 2 in English and Mathematics (DfES, 2006). Level 2 is noted by the Qualifications and Curriculum Authority (QCA) as the level necessary to 'participate in life, learning and work' (QCA, 2006).

The proficiency of students' language proved to be a key issue in my research for several reasons. In terms of the overall view of competence, there existed many different 'world views' within the different universes of thought and these viewpoints are explored in the book in subsequent chapters, but in terms of outlining the background here, the different entry qualifications of students and levels of language competence, meant that universities had to review their organisational structures and course contents (Archer, Hutchings and Ross, 2003; Davies, Williams and Webb, 1997; Wingate, 2007). As the new students have various levels of attainment and experience universities and HEIs had to look to different initiatives such as lowering their minimum entry qualifications, introducing short, preparatory pre-degree level study in the form of "summer school" type courses, and mentors for first year students (Thomas et al., 2003). A major strategy adopted by many universities was the establishment of centralised student support centres (SSCs). The general idea behind SSCs was that students could attend these facilities for optional, additional, generic help with their studies. In the late 1990s, this was a genuine idea, that had wide appeal, but ironically, the success of widening participation policies, was to shake this innocent idea to the core. The basic fact is that the idea of SSCs challenges the dominant assumption that every academic discipline has its own norms and procedures regarding approaches to writing and to the articulation of ideas (Gee, 2000; Hyland, 2004; Lea and Stierer, 2000; Monroe, 2002;).

Academic subject tutors, and even the same discipline subject tutors in the same programme of study have widely differing views of what constitutes an appropriate level of writing in any discipline. This issue is also further compounded by the different approaches subject tutors emphasise when they offer guidance to students on how they can acquire and develop knowledge in a discipline (Blythman and Orr 2002; Lillis, 2006). In a generic, multi-disciplinary cross institutional role, these differences are impossible to address within any fixed criteria, and/or learning outcomes. As academic writing at a higher level is not practical in isolation, the SSC tutor will offer guidance on writing style, at their own discretion. Any other help given, such as how to approach a particular assignment or whether a piece of work is of a high enough 'academic standard' for a course, is offered from the SSC tutor's own opinion from their 'world view' of how things are done in their subject within the discipline of their 'universe of knowledge'.

Becher (1989) and Becher and Trowler (2001) term these different disciplinary worlds *academic tribes* and I have argued in this book that the influence of these tribes is totally overlooked in views of how to help students succeed in higher education. I shall be discussing this influence in the book, but I note the point here, because it was completely ignored when SSCs were started in universities. I discuss the influence of government's higher education policies in the next chapter but it was universities response to the *Dearing Report* of 1997 that instigated the growth of SSCs. The next section, therefore, outlines the research study into an SSC, which forms the empirical evidence for the arguments made in this book.

The Research Study

The general idea then was that SSCs could help with all and everything to do with non-contextualised skills, but the research findings showed that this was never the case. The students attended the centre for the main reason that they wanted help with understanding their subject and how to write about it. As widening participation strategies employed by the researched university became more and more successful, the range of issues students presented to the staff in the SSC, also increased and diversified. Many students had both negative experiences of education or had been absent from it for one or more decades, although they were capable and keen to learn, they lacked confidence in knowing what and how to study at a higher level, and they did not know how to write about their subject. As students with such complex needs seemed to be increasing, I started the formal research. I commenced the longitudinal study by conducting a literature review and case study. The following six questions, therefore, formed the basis of the study:

1. What is the rationale for expanding access to HE?
2. What are the implications for the concept of a 'higher education'?
3. What is the literacy level/standard expected in HE?
4. Do students understand the level/standard of writing in HE?
5. Do levels of literacy and notions of standards differ across the disciplines?
6. Can students be supported to achieve the level of literacy required?
   (*Source*: Barkas, 2008).

I then applied an integrated methodology using both qualitative and quantitative research methods to conduct the research within a theoretical literacy framework. The results of the research encompass a complex set of ironies and paradoxes which were examined in the formal study. For example, on the one hand, management and academic staff were pleased they had a facility whereby students could be directed to obtain help with their studies. On the other hand, they did not want to acknowledge that this was a complex issue and that there was no such thing as a 'student's simple study problem' that could be solved with impartial, generic advice.

To write about the miscommunication over virtually every issue in the university, would be the topic of several other books, so in this book, I merely discuss how the contexts of the discourse of changing HE have compounded in the contradictory views of what SSCs can actually do.

Conclusion

In this chapter, I have set the context for the book and explained how and why the paradoxes and ironies of higher education can be conceptualised in the issues presented by SSCs. In their rush to meet governments' demands for widening participation, universities have become internally divided and fragmented organisations. This process is described by Winter (2009, 122) as "schisms". The management of the institutions have created their own worlds of 'double business speak', whilst openly competing against each other, yet the underlying text beneath their mission statements could be expressed as: 'we are selling education as a sort of product, but it's not really a product for sale, as we decide whether you can have it or not'. As the senior management play business games to justify their existence, the academic staff have almost to isolate themselves within their 'world of a subject' in their own 'tribe' (Becher and Trowler, 2001) to be able to meet the demands placed upon them, both by the diverse cohort of student intake and by the managers demanding evidence of success. This too, however, is not simply a binary conflict.

Some academics have moved away from teaching and research, becoming 'managers' with many embracing the system for their own career advancement, exploiting any opportunity or ignoring something that does not help them, as the case may be (Ainley 2000; Hager and Hodkinson 2009; Winter, 2009).

The practical impact on the 'here and now' in universities by the global nature of the complexity of different viewpoints is described by Nixon (2003, 5) as a "runaway world of increasing individualisation, and de-traditionalisation" whereby the managerialist solution is to "engage in restructuring exercises" which Nixon (2003, 8) says is analogous to "rearranging deckchairs" on a drowning vessel such as the *Titanic* when it hit an iceberg. The futility of trying to 'manage' explicitly, something such as 'learning' that is largely experienced implicitly, has done nothing to stop the onslaught of systems introduced to 'manage learning' (Henkel, 2000). Thus, opposing views can exist simultaneously in the same situation. For example, 'knowledge' and 'skills' are spoken of in merely rhetorical terms (Young, 2009) while there is no agreement on the meaning of the words. 'Knowledge' is accepted as a 'category' but its meaning is seen as implicit and virtually empty of content (Young 2009, 193) in some situations but even if the 'knowledge' in question is valued, it can be acquired at a low price. As trans-national corporations make up the 'global' economy, they can have their headquarters in one country but offices and businesses in many others. Thereby possessing a lead role in where they choose to situate work (Brown et al., 2008) so rather than knowledge being highly valued and desired and required at a high price, these companies can pay 'less for more.' This also translates into a global auction for jobs where knowledge is bought cheaply and 'low skilled jobs migrate to low-waged economies' (Brown et al., 2008). This employment situation represents what Brown et al., (2008) have argued is a shift in values from 'bloody wars to knowledge wars' with different corporations 'out-smarting' each other for huge profits in 'winner-takes all markets' (Frank and Cook 1996 quoted in Brown et al., 2008, 140). The reality of 'global economies' (Young 2009) makes for a very unstable 'market' for higher education as the 'level playing field' of know-ledge is 'ripped up' creating tensions in the different views between employers and universities (Brown et al., 2008 139). Universities have claimed they are providing 'knowledgeable graduates with 'skills' for employers but in light of the contradictions of values in global economics, three uncomfortable questions remain equally difficult to answer: what is this 'knowledge'? what 'skills' are provided? And which employers are the 'graduates' being prepared for? (Ainley, 2000; Brown et al., 2004; Young 2009; Young and Muller, 2010). These three questions require very careful clarification and definition before any answers can be presented. In 2010, the rhetoric continued but clarity of meaning and purpose remained elusive with viewpoints that appeared contradictory across the sector, resulting in tensions that can be depicted in the following two tables. Trying to find out who held the power in the university to address the misconceptions of skills and knowledge was like chasing a ghost, power appeared to be in a hidden place, seeming to be somewhere, but then appearing elsewhere (Ferguson, 1990, 9).

The first table presents the universal challenges to universities at the current time and the second table shows how these same challenges compound the issues presented by SSCs. The issues in the tables are all interwoven, both within and across all the others:-

Table 1. Universal challenges to universities

Holographic matrices of meanings

Different ideas about the role of universities on a global scale in the 21st century, expressed through the rhetorical use of terms such as:-

Skills – Knowledge - Employability – Marketisation ruled by the power of transnational companies to pay a low price for their view of 'knowledge' (Brown et al., 2008).

De-structuring of professionals (Beck and Young, 2005) along with a lack of agreement of what is meant by Skills (Unwin 2004b) and Knowledge versus Information (Young, 2009).

Growing use of the normalisation of genericism (Bernstein 2000) over knowledge & skills without 'content' (Nixon 2003; Winter 2009; Young 2009)

Rise of managerialism, the audit of 'systems' and 'management of learning (Henkel, 2000; Harvey, 2002).

These differentiated viewpoints can be demonstrated by the issues presented by research into the nature of queries in SSCs as shown in Table 2.

A complex and conflicting discourse can be exposed when the different meanings and use of the terms described in Tables 1 and 2 are evaluated. They show why SSCs became so widespread in post-1992 universities. The book, therefore, has been divided into 7 chapters. This chapter has presented the background to the issues that are examined further in later sections of the book. Chapter two presents an outline of the policy discourse that underlines the current complexity of issues in higher education. Chapter 3 shows how the different views of academic literacy are manifested in the discourse on skills and writing. Chapter 4 discusses the reasons why the role of teaching in SSCs is dismissed as 'low-level support'. A review of the research methodology and the study of the SSC is then presented in Chapter 5, with the discussion of the findings of the research following in Chapter 6. The concluding arguments then form the content of Chapter 7.

Table 2. The issues in academic literacy and the nature of the queries at SSCs

---

Confusion over what is meant by 'Student Support' as: cognitive, systemic or administrative? (Tait, 2000)

Academic literacy as: a skill; text based socialisation or practice based in social context (Barton 1994; Baynham 2000; Monroe 2002).

Skills as: study, key, core, basic or a mixture of the four (Ainley, 2000)

Differences in what is meant by 'good writing' and functional and/or academic literacy

Understanding learning versus constructing knowledge (Bernstein,2000; Young 2009)

Different views of teaching – teacher and content orientated or student and learner focussed (Kember, 1997)

Subject differences in the meaning of 'writing and knowledge', 'skills', 'support' and 'teaching' (Lea and Stierer, 2000)

Between the Text Comment

There is a tradition in academic writing that the writer must be objective and distant from the issue under study; to demonstrate objectivity and thereby allow the 'issues' to 'speak' for themselves without persuasive writing techniques. In normal academic writing purposes, such as essays and reports for course examination requirements, journal articles or formal reports, I fully support this view. While I have tried to conduct ethical and objective research, I was not able to 'walk away' from the study, because I was both an employee and researcher in the institution. A formal academic style of writing has been chosen for the main sections of the book, but as the research was conducted inside the university where I was employed, I hoped to encourage further reading of the book by adding the occasional 'between the text comment' . In these short sections, I would write in a personal style and include a little insight into something that happened during the research. A flight of fancy of the mind that is just a personal view; I offer the first of my little asides:

When I heard that the proposal for this book had been accepted, I was so thrilled that the story of the SSC could get into print, I thought the Director of the Library, (DL) would be pleased (my "line manager" at the time) - don't you dislike that term too? *Line-manager*? Are we all factory line computers now?

I can vividly recall the scene, it was a dark and stormy night … (not very imaginative, I know, but it was, honestly, a dark and stormy night) …well after 6.00pm and I knocked on the open office door. When the door was ajar, it was the DL's signal that members of staff could *drop-by*. The DL has been on the latest management courses, you see, so has learned they must at least, present the semblance of interest that the staff matter to them. It appears that the DL thinks they work in a trans-national firm or corporate finance, not a library, but let's not split hairs. I knocked on the door...and I took the grim look of suppressed pain on the DL's face, as the expression of welcome. I said I was the bearer of good news and that I was thrilled to let them know, I had secured a book contract to write about the SSC! You know the little corner of the library on the ground floor where students congregate? The glazed look in the DL's eyes, gave them away, behind a half-hearted "well done, that's very good", (but run along now, I am busy, I have forms to fill in) made me realise that the DL spoke for their colleagues. I could almost feel the DL's thoughts. Yes, this little SSC *Skills Only* person may think she has something to say, but no-one is interested, so they won't buy or ever read her little, insignificant book. I wish she would stop bothering me. Besides, we, *the managers* (let's not forget we make the decisions around here) are not going to give in to her and let her back into an academic team, we have a skills and employability agenda to adhere to and we have the power. It's in our five and ten year plans and that's it now. *We* decide.

"…I just thought I would let you know, I will be off now." I resisted the temptation to add – *well, I'll go back under my rock then*? The DL might be right, but what worried me the most was, I thought librarians liked books? I suppose they want 'virtual libraries' now, so where is the place for the human writer? As I returned to my office, I felt once again, the all too familiar feeling of despair. What has happened to higher education, when form filling and future planning are more important than meeting students' needs in the 'now'? How can opinions about roles have become so divided? Who was making the decisions? In the course of the research, I was left with the impression that the managers refused to acknowledge the complexity of the SSC, simply because they could. For what other reason would they ignore the wealth and depth of the evidence? There was, after all, 12 years of it?

End of Comment

I now return to the formal style.

The following chapter outlines the policy development that has created the 'multi-verses' of these parallel universes and attempts to show how they have manifested in practical terms in SSCs.

NOTES

[1] This book focuses on higher education in England, but it is important to note here that the UK government's 'widening participation' agenda is being pursued in Scotland, Wales and Northern Ireland. Due to devolved powers to the different parts of the UK, different policies and strategies are emerging.

THE DIMENSIONS THROUGH TIME OF THE FRAMEWORK OF WIDENING PARTICIPATION

INTRODUCTION

The use of an analogy in the form of the analytical metaphor of 'multiverse' (Chown, 2007) provides a way of showing how the differentiated discourse of widening participation in higher education creates complex and contradictory views that exist simultaneously. The resistance to accepting an alternative view is so strong that conflict often has to arise before any change or progress can be made. The examples offered provide aerial views of the different dimensions of viewpoints that then create challenges for all those involved in higher education. These 'snapshots', in turn, offer an explanation as to how and why the contested opinions of what is meant by 'teaching and/or supporting' students gained favour in universities attempting to meet widening participation targets.

Within the multiple-parallel universes, five broad dimensions can be identified. Then, as in a symbolic hologram, within these five dimensions are five worlds of influence and together, they can therefore, provide a Foucauldian (1972) 'pantopian' outlook of the key aspects of conceptual frameworks which have influenced higher education's development over the past few decades. Each of these 'conceptual worlds' is immense with extensive literature on every aspect of the area, so the purpose in this book, is simply to provide some snapshots in time to highlight how and why, they were instrumental in bringing about the divisive nature of current thinking about teaching in higher education. These viewpoints in turn, underpin the attitudes of management and staff towards why, in their beliefs, they remain convinced that 'skills' without a given context can be taught in SSCs.

The five dimensions all are interwoven to a greater or lesser degree, so my boundaries are very much, symbolic and fluid barriers. I offer them to you in this separated form, merely to allow for a clearer line of discussion. The dimensions involve and reflect, the 'worlds of influence' within the 'parallel universes' that make up the views of higher education. I decided that I could examine five of the main areas that have affected the work of SSCs, and during my search of the literature, I found these to be: policy discourse; the changing role of universities; human capital theories and social capital theories; lifelong learning and access.

The dimensional concepts are discussed extensively from within and across different subjects and disciplines and in numerous contexts. Although the concepts are frequently grouped together, for the purpose of discussion to help clarify the closest related issues that influence the work in SSCs and therefore, universities generally, I have subsequently, grouped the issues across five columns and five rows as shown in Table 4 below. The differentiating arguments arising from these five concepts, creates challenges in seven main areas of universities' higher educational provision. Each of the different views of how best to address the issues in the topic creates tensions across all the other areas, and although the 'dimension' may make perfect sense to its believers in one 'world of thought', it is not acknowledged or even understood from a different viewpoint within the context of another 'world', from another standpoint in the discourse. For example, the vertical column 'widening access' is discussed from each of the other topics in the other four columns and also from the four topics in the 5 rows. The other 2 of the 7 issues which are 'demands of governments and employers (Key Skills, later called employment (or employability) skills in the 2000s, and Graduateness) and 'discourse of language and literacy' influence the different arguments from the issues shown in all the 5 columns and 5 rows.

Table 3. Dimensions and influence - worlds within worlds in the multiverse of higher education; students skills centres and widening participation

5 Dimensions	5 Worlds of influence
Academic literacy	Policy Discourse
Skills	Changing Role of Universities
Knowledge	Human and Social Capital Theories
Business & technology	Lifelong Learning
Teaching	Access (*Source*: Barkas 2008).

Table 4. The 7 areas of tension involved in creating widening participation in higher education

1. Demands of governments and employers (key skills then employment skills and 'graduateness')				
(3) Widening Participation & Access	(4) Debates about the effects of policies	(5) University teaching/ research staff-peer evaluation	(6) Quality Assurance	(7) Students - writing & study skills
Community education	Management of universities	Curriculum change & academic literacy	Subject Reviews	Social Background
Access to FE	Business of education	Maintenance of standards	Administration of Higher Education	Preparation for HE
Access to HE	Learning materials	Methods of assessment & Skills development	Internal and External Audits	Inclusion/ exclusion
Return to learn/study courses	Marketing of institutions/ Courses	Student Support	Theories of Teaching and learning	Choice/mix of course
Accredited Leisure Courses v. NVQs	Information Technology	Knowledge-what is it?	Research	Students' expectations & career aims
2. Discourse of language and literacy				

Source: Barkas (2008).

The categories 1 and 2 - 'Demands of governments and employers (Key Skills and *Graduateness*)' and 'discourse of language and literacy' form tacit, underlying threads through all the other 5 categories, but it is possible to read arguments in the literature about widening participation's role in higher education that are written from one perspective and do not necessarily mention these two influences or any part of the other areas. There are, therefore, potentially 32 broad areas of debate in the literature, which does not take into account the different layers of discussion possible in any one of the categories. The seven broad categories are interwoven, overlapping to a greater or lesser extent.

Each of the five dimensions: academic literacy; knowledge; skills, business and technology and teaching run in strands through all discussions through the seven categories. They are depicted in Table 4, in lines across and down in the columns and rows, where they frequently appear in 'lines of reasoning', in any given argument; but of course, they can be discussed from, or within, any of the other categories. For example, a central issue for the researched SSC, was that the Human Resource Managers claimed that the work in the SSC was a 'support' role, 'supporting students' 'skills' and apparently, no academic knowledge was needed to do this.

The literature on any one of the areas in the table is very important. It is also extensive and heavily detailed, so my divisions and categories are offered merely to illustrate the arguments from within the context of my analytical metaphor to demonstrate how the unrealistic expectations about the role of SSCs, has gradually developed and therefore intensified through each encounter or influence. By this, I mean that the ideas about how the SSC worked would appear in various documents that indirectly came my way. Such as feedback comments on students work, where they were told to come to the SSC for help. They are offered in this simple form for clarity, not to diminish their effect, which can be profound.

Between the Text Comment

What do we know of PSR 1913 + 16 (PSR stands for Pulsar) or the shortest path from A to B in three dimensions? (Hawking, 1988, 90 and 163). Not a lot, but probably more than we did before the SSC opened. Or are they lost in Black holes? "Did you know that a black hole is a region of space where gravity is so strong that not even light, the fastest thing in the Universe, can escape" (Chown 2007, 28). You see, SSCs are really little black holes in space. The staff cannot escape, well not unless Captain Spock of the Star Ship Enterprise was to come in and beam us all up to a different world. Wonder if I need to find a reference for Spock? Perhaps not as the phrase and images have become part of our discourse, but just in case here is one: (Startreck.com 2010).

Back to the Text

I have therefore, separated this chapter into the five areas of influence: policy discourse; the changing role of universities; human and social capital theories; life-long learning and access to discuss how the five dimensions of: academic literacy;

skills; knowledge; business and technology and teaching are viewed and articulated from quite different perspectives. Of course, the discourse of language and literacy makes up all the *language* of all the areas of *influence* and the *dimensions,* but I have chosen to write more specifically about the issues in 'academic literacy' and 'language' in chapter 3. The five major areas of influence are now discussed in the following section, starting with 'policy discourse'.

Policy Discourse

Over the past five decades, there have been seven major policy developments for higher education (See Table 5).

Table 5. The major policy documents for higher education in England

Year	Education policy	Focus
1963	Robbins' Report	Creation of new universities
1991	Education and Training for the 21st Century	Emphasis on vocational education
1992	Further and Higher Education Reform Act	Abolished binary divide, polytechnics became universities
1997	Kennedy Report	Widening Participation in Further Education
1997	Dearing Report	Widening Participation in Higher Education
1997	Fryer Report	Widening access by focus on social exclusion groups
2004	The Future of Higher Education	'Graduateness' and Economic Rationality. (*Source*: Barkas, 2008).

Student support or skills centres, started in higher education, as senior managers attempted to respond quickly to the Dearing Report's (1997) policy emphasis for widening participation, but the differentiated discourse, can be traced to the Robbins Report (1963). There is extensive literature about all these policies (see inter-alia, Ainley, 2000; Barnett, 1994; Coffield, 1998) but the current complexity and contradiction in the reality of universities today, can therefore be attributed to the effects of these policies. For illustration, I have chosen to briefly describe two 'snapshots' in time, the impact of the Robbins Report (1963) and the conflicting views of vocational education in the 1980s. Of course, this is not to suggest that the impact of the other policies was of any less importance. I have simply chosen these examples because they encapsulate all the other tensions in the development of higher education that have developed for over the past five decades.

It is possible to argue that the greatest change to thinking about the role of universities, commenced after the Robbins Report (1963). Perhaps it is Barnett (1994, 4) who succinctly expresses the major change for higher education, when he said this report was the "...last of the great liberal statements of higher education".

Barnett (ibid, 18) has suggested that "...unwittingly, Robbins marked the end of a transitional era, in which higher education was seen as a cultural or positional good, rather than an economic good". It is the focus on the *economics* of a university education that was to start the change of emphasis in the discourse of higher education provision.

The Robbins Report stressed that barriers to educational achievement were not genetic but social. The four aims of the Report, did argue for useful labour skills, but not without the advancement of learning and the development of the intellect. These were to be achieved within the transmission of a common culture and standards of citizenship. It is, therefore, possible to argue that these aims for higher education are as important today as over forty years ago. This is mainly because students desiring a university education have to be ever more flexible and resourceful to cope with the changing nature and structure of career and employment opportunities as a result of globalisation and information technology. At one time, a degree qualification was sufficient to secure entry into professional occupations (Halsey, 1992). Writing reflectively some time after the main recommendations of the report were accepted, Robbins (1980) was alarmed that the report was not being accepted in its truest sense, and aspects of it were being used out of context, so in an attempt to redress the balance, he stressed that the report was the joint work of the committee members but the main aim of the work 'opening up access to universities' was to be become known as the 'Robbins' principle'. He stressed the importance of universities in developing the "...powers of the mind" (ibid, 6), acknowledging the central importance of research and teaching together in one institution, arguing that these are critical and "...tangible functions we look for in universities" (ibid, 7). Robbins (1980) was keen to maintain 'intellectual standards' saying that in the pursuit of knowledge students must learn how to acquire the skills of acquisition, but not necessarily through too much early specialisation in schools or academic subjects. His view was for schools to concentrate on a broad range of subjects, leaving specialisation to the universities, arguing that students do not develop all their learning capabilities in a linear fashion. This view, in part, was connected to his opinion that democratic and liberal civilisations must not be 'dogmatic and intolerant' (ibid, 9). These four aims have been extensively examined in the literature (see inter alia, Barnett, 1990; 1994; Edwards et al 2002; Field, 2002; Halsey, 1995; Scott, 1998), but two important inferences are at the centre of the differing perspectives on widening participation in higher education; first, the role of universities and, second, access to universities.

The first inference relates to one of the roles of a university, which is 'instruction in skills suitable to play a part in the general division of labour' and the second is more broadly related to the 'access' students' profile (Armstrong, 2000). As Coffield (1998, 51) explains:

Investment in education and training is necessary but not a sufficient condition of sustained economic prosperity; the point is neatly captured in the phrase "Let them eat skills." This exhortation is the title of an article by Douglas Noble (1994, 22, quoted in Coffield, 1998, 51) who argues that in the USA and in the UK, the wages and job security of those still employed are steadily eroding, as organised labour has been all but destroyed, and most new jobs are in the low-wage, temporary, part-time, service sector, requiring minimal skills. The result may be a highly skilled elite and a growing army of the (at best) semi-skilled and expendable.

The central issue here is that the problems in changing patterns of work are not just about skills deficits. This issue relates directly to the questions about universities' role in society but as explained by Coffield (1998, 55), "...change today is so rapid, ubiquitous, unpredictable and inescapable that attention to it tends to eclipse consideration of deep continuities, traditional inequalities and new forms of economic polarisation". In terms of the relationship of skill training and employment opportunities and whether or not a university education could have a direct 'cause and effect' relationship, Robbins (1980, 10) was adamant that this link could not be empirically proven:

> I simply cannot take seriously any attempt to trace any obvious correlation between rates of growth of national product – however this nebulous quantity is measured – and all the proportion of the relevant age-groups receiving higher education. Needless to say, there must be some correlation between the proportion of highly trained engineers and the prevalence of successful industry attending their operations...but I should be greatly surprised if, outside specific vocational correlations of the sort, anything much wider and as tangible could be found; the variables are so numerous and the connections are so often indirect.

In the 1960s and early 1970s, Robbins and his colleagues could not have predicted the growing influence over four decades of market-based economics and their heavy influence in changing society's general expectations of its universities' role in providing skilled workers to ensure competitiveness in international trade. It is not unrealistic to claim, however, that the marketisation of universities has dramatically changed the nature of higher education (Beck and Young, 2005; Newman and Jahdi, 2009). Higher education today has to justify its courses in terms of 'value' for the economy but over thirty years ago, the binary system of universities and technical colleges, which latterly became polytechnics, still had split functions. Universities provided a higher 'academic education', and the higher technical colleges (polytechnics) more generally, provided vocational training such as engineering. Robbins (1963, 1980) was to argue that he saw no reason why good technical education could not be provided in universities, citing several successful European establishments as possible models.

The second inference of the Robbins' report (Robbins, 1963), which is directly related to the current different interpretations of 'access' to higher education, is the profile of the mature student. Robbins, (ibid, 23) recommended that places at university "… should be available to all who have the ability and willingness to benefit from them". Their one condition was that universities should offer a broader range of courses. The complex nature of the challenges involved in defining and quantifying what is meant by 'the ability and willingness to benefit' continues to be a contentious issue in the literature on widening participation. Coffield and Vignoles (1997) have argued that: "It is worth recalling that the Robbins Report firmly rejected the notion of a "so-called pool of ability" (Robbins, 1963, para 137).

Robbins' (ibid) argued that he did not believe that the number of people who could benefit from a higher education was limited to a small number or "pool". He stressed that many people develop their "abilities" at different times and stages in their lives and this process was not fixed. Other researchers, such as Crowther (2004) and Armstrong, (2000), have argued that the ability and willingness to benefit is also not straightforward.

At the time of the Robbins committee's proposals, attention was on encouraging the old universities to offer places to those who were termed 'non-traditional students'. This was taken to mean those students who did not necessarily have high grades in GCE A levels, or did not come from private schools, or from the wealthier 'middle classes' as social-economic groups one and two (Archer et al., 2003) were termed at the time. Robbins (1963, 1980) was to argue that providing more places was no threat to maintaining high academic standards. The 'ability and willingness to benefit' from a university place is also at the centre of the current discourse on the changing role of universities. To whom 'access' is offered is where different emphasis on the term lies. Directly related to 'willingness to benefit' is that the cost of a higher education is now partially expected from subsidised contributions in the form of loans, instead of grants, to students. Although students do not start to pay back these loans until after their income reaches a specified level, the principle behind their introduction, does reflect the changing nature of higher education in the 21st century. In the 1960s, a university education was subsidised and students could apply for a means tested grant through their local education authority. Robbins (1980), however, predicted that financing wider access to higher education would involve a review of investment and did not discount the need for students' contri-butions, basing his views on the work of a public finance expert at the time, Professor Prest (cited in Robbins, 1980, 35). Prest (ibid, 35) supported the idea of loans rather than subsidies to students, arguing that "...re-payment shall only be required if subsequent earnings pass beyond a figure which makes reasonable interest and amortisation possible". This scheme seemed practical to Robbins (1980) because it did not require a separate bureaucracy to administer it as the monies could be managed through the existing workings of the Inland Revenue.

In the last economic downturn in the 1980s, policy attention focussed on 'skills'. In the 1980s, the discourse on skills and competencies gained momentum and was reflected in the moves for more vocationally related courses in the polytechnics. Barnett (1994, 68) explains:

Vocationalism is not as value-free as it would pretend. It is an ideology represen-ting the interests of corporatism, of economy and of profit. Vocationalism asserts the desirability of a fit between higher education and the world of work and of graduates being enterprising in it.

The use of the term *vocationalism* is therefore, highly contested. In terms of skills development, however, the term *vocational* can be applied in a more positive sense to mean development in the crafts, technical or professional levels (Jessup, 1990;

Bates, 1997; Coffield and Williamson, 1997; Unwin, 2004a). In the context of educational change, the discourse of 'vocationalism' is at the centre of the debate of higher education's role in the dispersal of knowledge in society, which in effect has changed from "...higher education in society to higher education of society" (Barnett, 1994, 6). Unwin, (2004a, 175) has argued that despite the importance of a vocational education in governments' legislation, "... the United Kingdom's approach to vocational education is more confused and impoverished than ever." This is because of long standing, unwarranted prejudice as to the value of vocational against academic education (Bligh 1990).

This prejudice is shown in the nature of the language which reflects the struggles policy makers and/or educationists have in locating vocational training. Unwin (2004a, 177) argues that while UK governments' policies continually stress the need for more skills, there is not a consensus view of how this can be achieved:

> Over the past 150 years in the UK, numerous committees have grappled with the question of whether general or academic education should be kept separate from or integrated with vocational education, and often in isolation, with the parallel problem of the UK's lack of robust technical education.

The contradictions are reflected in the nature of the discourse of vocational education, whereby its critics have argued that there was a fundamental 'dishonesty' in what became known as the *New Vocationalism* of the 1970s (Stronach and MacLure, 1997; Unwin, 2004a, 182). Stronach and MacLure (ibid, 87) note how the discourse of vocationalism is applied and interpreted differently depending on the context of its use from "...translations in ideology, policy, programme and practice". Coffield (1998, 58) for example, showed how the colourful language used to describe the vocational course masked the lack of content they actually contained. In other words, training schemes of variable credibility were set up to attract students for 'skills training' for jobs that often did not exist, they were just an attempt made by the government to 'up-skill' the unemployed (Fuller and Unwin, 2001; Hyland, 2003; Parry, 2005; Unwin and Wellington, 2001).

Despite these early failures, the emphasis on 'skills' however they may be defined in any specific context, has dominated government policy. The language of 'skills' is really a 'world within a world' and searching for definitions and clarity without ambiguity becomes nothing more than a chimera hunt; this has not stopped governments or universities management marketing the idea of 'skills', but without saying exactly what they are. The loose rhetoric then ends up energising itself and it just continues, and in 2010, this 'language of skills' was the nature of the umbrella term 'employability'. Beck et al., (1994) define this process as 'de-traditionalisation' within a 'risk' society. This is because of the marketing of products, and education is included in this. The same methods are applied; for example, constructed within the internet, but this is also alongside the same uncertainty and insecurity of any 'market'. The marketing of higher education takes place because of the reports and legislation that have been introduced amongst policies of privatisation, within competition driven systems of competitive tendering and contracting; that are an attempt to develop accountable public services that are effective and efficient

(Pollitt and Bouckaert, 2002). These policies have instigated competition between universities, alongside performance measurement targets which have been further criticised for their excessive bureaucratic procedures (Meek, 2000).

The 'parallel worlds' of the policy discourse gains momentum over time but then continues to be entrenched with opposing and contradictory values and meanings, that move and change extensively through different time periods. For example, although the word 'access' is frequently used in the context of 'widening participation', to mean access to higher education, it is also used to refer to access to adult and continuing education and also as 'Access' with a capital 'A' to mean an accredited or non-accredited Access to Higher Education Course (Davies, et al., 1997; Parry, 1995; Parry et al., 2004). During the past decade, widening participation has gradually replaced the term 'widening access' to higher education, which was used in the 1963 Robbins Report (HMSO, 1963). The use of widening participation as a policy term started when the government announced its National Learning Target in 1999 for 50 per cent of participation by young people (18–30) in higher education institutions by 2010 and this was followed by a target for 2020 of over 90 per cent of the working age population to be skilled up to level 2 or higher, 68 per cent to be level 3 or above and over 40 per cent to be level 4 (BIS 2009, 6). The target has been extensively criticised in the literature (see inter alia: Coates and Adnett, 2002; D'Andrea and Gosling, 2005; Ganobcsik-Williams, 2006; Rikowski, 2001). Other writers focus their arguments more on the divisive nature of the introduction of tuition fees, which could act as a further barrier to access and have a direct effect on participation (see inter alia, Glennerster, 2002; Powley, 2001). Hager and Hodkinson's (2009) research examines the nature of the polarised attitudes to learning in higher education and Young's (2009) research examines the different attitudes to knowledge.

The 'what' and 'how' universities were going to meet the needs of so many more students, has only been given surface attention. Intrinsic to this problem is the lack of attention that has been given to the first principle of 'inclusion' in widening access. A key aspect of widening participation that is also highly debated in the specialist literature is the fact that today's students entering universities grew up amongst the efforts to provide inclusive education, "in addition to the general trend towards inclusive education, HEFCE have recognised the importance of supplementary provision for students with disabilities" (Hayes, 1997, 258). As in schools and colleges, inclusive education has also become part of the curriculum in higher education institutions, with many universities providing specialist units to ascertain the special needs of these learners (Hayes, ibid). The researched university has a separate, specialist unit which is called the "Disability and Specific Learning Difficulties" Unit (that was its name at the start of 2009, but I had heard another title was to be introduced). So although the students are 'included' in the university, there is an additional unit to support their learning needs. This unit is separate to the SSC, but the students also make use of the SSC's services.

This whole concept of being part of higher education but then having extra and/or special help challenges the notion of social inclusion; there are therefore, a number of inherent difficulties involved in conceptualising the contexts of inclusion and exclusion policies. Widening participation in higher education is part of social inclusion policies, but, as argued by Slee (2001, 168), the inclusion policies both for schools and universities cover up a "fundamental cultural flaw" because the fact that students with special learning needs are segregated or given different help, is not "inclusion". Slee (ibid) argued "inclusion is an aspiration for a democratic education, and, as such, the project of inclusion addresses the experiences of all students". He goes on to argue that "teacher education needs to explore new forms of knowledge about identity and difference and to suggest new questions that invite students to consider the pathologies of schools that enable or disable students" (Slee, 2001, 174). Here, the loose language of widening participation is given practical physicality. That is, if a student in higher education is seen to have "special learning needs" what criteria would denote the *special-ness* and how would this impact on the *none-special-ness* of other students? As identified by Slee (2001) these are un-comfortable questions that do need addressing from an empirical stand point. This argument is particularly important when examining the role of SSCs. If SSCs are seen as a necessary *addition* to the higher education curriculum, how then can their remit be evaluated and against what? I will return to this issue in the next chapter but I note it here to show how the policy discourse glosses over key points, when definition and clarification should have been established before the policy was conceptualised.

The term *widening participation* is also used randomly in the discourse; perhaps with somewhat less, delicate connotations; or because the contradictions in the applica-tion of the term are not openly confronted. Widening participation is generally used to describe the furthering of students' access opportunities to education, and higher education in particular. The definitions, however, behind the use of the term, are used in various contexts within differing theoretical perspectives of the role of higher education in contemporary society. The purpose of this section of the chapter is to examine the use of the term widening participation from some of these differing viewpoints. Policies on widening participation in higher education raise two sets of questions:

1. What are the best ways for universities to open up their access opportunities to a more diverse cohort of students?
2. How do governments of western democracies see the need to change the nature of a higher education to comply with employer demands?

These two questions are set against a background of policies based on the concept of "knowledge based economies" (KBEs), whose advent, Brown and Hesketh, (2004, 47) argue, "… lies in the shift from an unskilled or low skilled economy to one based on high skills and high wages". For the past decade the discourse of 'employability' has become so prevalent in the media that it appears, there is never enough time to stop and question the practical ways this KBE, could, if it exists, be created. The rhetoric of knowledge workers/knowledge economy is aglow with positive statements, as encapsulated by Brown and Hesketh (2004, 1) as "smart people, in smart jobs, doing smart things, for smart money, increasingly open to all rather than a few". Their research, however, into occupational stratification in the United States and Europe, showed that there were not enough of these high profile jobs to meet the demand. The over-inflation of the idea of a highly knowledgeable workforce is also challenged from other writers, such as Leadbetter (1999) when he said that any "economy" is the sum of many different workers' contributions, who together, allow people to live 'wealthy' lives. To enable people to live, they have to have the support of a vast array of workers from service industry employees, to farmers and butchers, electricians, to plumbers, carpenters and bricklayers. As Leadbetter's (1999) book title suggest, "people do not live on thin air". The belief in the idea that more 'skilled' workers will therefore mean more a more economically competitive economy falls flat when the supply of graduate employment seems to run dry (Brown and Hesketh, 2004). The hyperbolism of knowledge based economies conveniently ignores the key issue in employment patterns that can be both "relative" and "absolute" as the same time (Brown and Hesketh, 2004, 43). Policy debates tend to be "absolute" and focus on how workers can develop skills for the job market, without fully acknowledging how this skill base is changeable and "relative" to individuals and a fluctuation job market, as the global recession that started in 2008 has shown. This issue is aggravated still further, as regardless of how the employment trends move, there is a fundamental dilemma in finding agreed definitions of what is meant by "high skills" (Brown, Green and Lauder, 2001, 57).

For example, *high skills* can equally mean specialist technical skills and knowledge or generic competencies (such as IT, communications and problem solving). The problems associated with defining exactly what is required by these two questions, therefore, results in what Brown et al., (ibid, 137) has named "pressure points and trade offs" in what they describes as four resulting areas of conflict:

> Specifically there are four sets of contradictions or tensions which define the boundaries of policy making in the current United Kingdom context. These can be stated as the tensions between (1) company profitability and national prosperity; (2) flexible labour markets and social partnerships; (3) high-technology and intermediate technology manufacturing and services; and (4) more generally between economic and social priorities.

In 2008, the start of a global economic downturn made the talk of the "knowledge economy" sound hallow and brittle. The start of the collapse was created by over ambitious risk management strategies by international banks, such as Lehman Brothers investment bank (Duncan, 2008). Despite its flaws, the belief in KBEs has gained support during the marketisation of higher education over the past four decades. Research by Brown Green and Lauder (2008) however, provides evidence to challenge the claims about KBEs because their findings showed that transnational corporations do not make the market decisions on human capital theories on which KBEs are based. These new, very powerful global corporations do require 'knowledge workers' but the sort of employee they are seeking is a knowledgeable highly skilled specialist in a specific field that depends on the nature of the business of the trans-national corporation. This creates a situation that Brown et al., (2008, 140) describe as a replace-ment of "knowledge wars over bloody wars" (see also Human Capital theories below).

In summary, the current tension in higher education can basically be shown by the example of two opposing theories. These are the views that fall into one of two overarching themes as explained by Stewart Ranson, (1998) and Christopher Ball, (1990). Ranson (1998) has argued that a learning society should demonstrate a democratic and moral order that is not just economically driven, whereas Ball (1990) argued the opposite, saying that learning is individuals' responsibility in a competitive economic environment. The 'New Labour' government of 1997, followed the theme of Ball (ibid) over Ranson (1998) and continued to base its educational policies on the needs of the economy (Coffield, 1998; Tomlinson, 2001) and for another decade up to 2009, has continued to do so.

Looking back over the past four or five decades it is possible to see the contradictions in the policy discourse quite clearly. Governments' welfare based education policies have slowly changed, to be replaced with what Beck et al., (1994) have termed "reflexive modernisation" which means, rather than the government, it is the individual's responsibility to find employment. This change of thought was first shown in the 1970s when the emphasis on technical education in polytechnics, contradicted the monetarist doctrine adopted by the Conservative governments at the time. This started a series of cuts in public expenditure that continued into the 1980s and full tuition fees for international students were introduced (Kogan and Kogan, 1983; Scott, 1998) whereby critics of the government's policies coined the term 'Thatcherism', arguing that these restrictive practices 'masqueraded' behind a public face of 'democratic and liberal approaches to education' (Whitty, 2002, 19). It is possible to agree with these accusations, because the government appeared simply to want to save money, without apparently considering the long-term implications. A series of cuts to universities was imposed, which was to have a long-term effect on higher education. Less money meant more competition for fewer places, and the recession of the late 1970s and early 1980s meant high unemployment (Green, 1997). A particular irony of the financial restraints of support to universities was that the Conservative government cut funds to science, technology and other vocational courses, by 20% (Bligh, 1990, 42), while the current government is insisting that these are the same areas that need more graduate employees to raise Britain's competitive standing in global markets.

This "economic rationalisation" (Duke, 2002, 4) is based on skills' deficit models (Crowther, 2000, 2004) which then embraces the ideals of corporate business. Although convincing on the surface, this is not an appropriate approach for universities because while universities have to change to manage some market demands, they are also unique organisations. If a key role for universities is *new knowledge* a further function is also about the "continuity, conservation and transmission of understanding knowledge and values" (Duke, 2002, 7). The government's demands to ensure economic success again manifested with the introduction of employer related foundation degrees. Foundation degrees are a further attempt by the government to encourage more direct links with employers to "up-skill" the workforce by encouraging more vocationally relevant qualifications (HEFCE, 2001). It was hoped that the start of foundation degrees would help continue the move to widening participation in HEIs. The concept of widening participation fits with the New Labour concept of, the 'Third Way' (Fairclough, 2000a; Giddens, 1998).

The 'third way' was an attempt to direct policies into a middle line approach that combined the best of social and free market policies (Giddens, 1998). The influence of the 'third way' concept meant that government viewed social policy as an arena in which the different aspects of public life (education, health, crime and welfare) would be much more strongly connected. New Labour saw the country's economic success as processing through "...a learning policy of 'Foundation' and 'Lifelong Learning', linked to an active benefits system" (Ainley, 1999, 1). Ainley, (ibid) challenges the reality of a possible 'third way':

> There is no 'third way' between the state and the market', or the European and American models of capitalism, and New Labour is committed to the latter. In the new Americanised mixed economy of semi-privatised state and state-subsidised private sectors, New Labour 'stakeholdings' by private capital investment inpublic services represent a dominance of private over state monopoly capital (Ainley, 1999, 2).

Giddens (1998, 80) described this process as '...an increasingly reflexive society, which is also marked by high levels of self-organisation'. He supports this point by saying that the renewal of a 'civil society' will be by the cooperation of multi-agencies working in partnerships. Whilst agreeing with Giddens, in principle, I would support Ainley's (1999) view and also argue that this ideal does not sufficiently discuss the theoretical, practical and operational problems in reconciling a working relationship that crosses the different cultures and philosophies of these 'multi-agencies.' The different bureaucratic structures of these 'multi-agencies' often cause communication problems, both theoretically and structurally, as identified by researchers examining how far widening participation in HE has been achieved. For example, Reynolds, (2003) had to embrace the different cultures of the Health Service and Social Services when examining widening participation in neighbourhood renewal projects and Powley (2001) discovered how complex and problematic multi-agency relationships are between different agencies when she tried to examine the scale of widening participation in Cumbria.

A renewal of 'civil society' can only be achieved when more attention is given to the essence of the value of 'education' as social capital which is because 'learning is quintessentially social' (Coffield, 1998, 46). As Hyland (2003, 127) has stressed there must be a real cultural 'social vision' that appreciates education as a "public good", which is based on a principle of trust, grounded in fairness at all levels of society. For a higher education to have a value that is more than employment orientated there must be mechanisms in place to ensure that each generation is given the opportunity to study cultural and social knowledge. For this to work, as Hyland, (1998) and Giddens (1998) and others, have argued, policies must be directed to allow this to take place.

The possibility of social justice aims succeeding over the next decade are hindered by the continuing, and very real, problem of poverty in urban and rural Britain. Many of the initiatives such as 'Sure Start'[1] (Reynolds, 2003) emphasise the importance of addressing the issues of poverty, unemployment and crime in these areas, before participation in any education programme can be attempted.

Reynolds, (2003) suggests caution when referring to social exclusion zones. The term 'social exclusion', however, has been criticised for the way it has been conceptualised (Archer, 2001). Archer (2001) argues that the people who are 'excluded' are written about in a negative way, without sufficient attention being made to multiple in-equalities in the way participation in education is portrayed. This point is further discussed below in relation to who has access to universities. The next section explains how the role of higher education has changed through the policy discourse.

Higher Education's Changing Role in Society

The long term impact of the legislative changes imposed on HEIs is difficult to quantify. HEIs are attempting to address the challenges currently presented by 'widening access' to a higher education, but, before any real impact into 'widening participation' can be achieved, there must be a period of legislative stability to allow universities to consolidate the existing knowledge of access issues and form long term plans on how best to meet them. I would, therefore, support the arguments raised over a decade ago by Stronach and Morris (1994, 6) whose phrase 'policy hysteria' was used to explain the 'frenetic' and contradictory nature of the educational reforms over the past twenty years. Stronach and Morris (ibid, 6) show how this 'policy hysteria' was created, for example, by "…frequent policy switches, involving inconsistent aims and means"…"erosion of professional discretion by centralising control"… and "untested and un-testable claims".

In a later work on the application of the discourse of post-modernism to educational research, Stronach and MacLure (1997, 88) extend the support of these earlier criticisms by showing how government policies have created tensions in educational reform. For example, they show how another policy initiative has been introduced before an evaluation of the previous one has been possible:

> UK educational change in the 1980s and 1990s was characterized by recurring waves of reform…Multiple innovation became the norm, with the next set of reforming initiatives overtaking and overlapping the last before their effect was known or knowable…the same government led the charge towards basic skills in 1980, and away again in 1984. The government supported 'generic competencies' in 1984 and reverted to basic subjects and standards in 1988. Records of achievement became the hitch hiker of the educational galaxy, forever being picked up and put down in a different place – as a vocational guide, as personal development, as curriculum vitae, as a counselling instru-ment, as individual action planning. Traditional values were the problem in 1989 and the solution in 1993.

This indecision over policy recurred again in the 1990s and 2000s as people's skills were polarised, up-skilled or de-skilled; lack of 'skills' was still problematic in 1999 but employees had to be 'high skilled' by 2009 (Ainley, 2000; Gallie, 1994; Young and Muller, 2010). As the role of higher education in society has changed over time, I would argue that five periods can be identified as marking the point when the meaning and role of higher education took a different turn (See Table 6).

Table 6. The key periods in higher education history

ERA	Concept of higher education
Medieval England	Vocational
John Henry Newman 1865	Liberal education and the 'idea of a university'
Robbins 1963	Meritocracy and access
Post 1992	Vocational Skills
Post 2004	Struggling for identity

The philosophical meaning of the role of a 'university' is strongly debated in the educational literature. For example, Leavis (1965) has maintained that universities are critical to the preservation of 'knowledge' in what he calls "higher culture" in society. This culture, stemming from John Henry Newman's work in "The Idea of a University" in the mid-nineteenth century, was in essence the pursuit of truth and knowledge (Elliott, 2004). Newman's claim was that there was more to education than training for work, his emphasis was for a liberal education, which by itself can make "a cultivated intellect, a delicate taste, a candid, equitable, dispassionate mind" (Newman, 1852, 5 quoted in Elliott, 2004, 1). Bligh (1990) has identified three fundamental influences on the role of British universities. These influences in western civilisations are represented by the Church, the State and universities (ibid, 22), which have had a long standing critical impact on how knowledge is interpreted and valued:

> From Galilee it obtained religion, many of its moral principles, its national and domestic rituals, its community focus, the stability of the family and its softer values including its service to others..., from Rome it inherited the basis of its laws, the foundations of its government, its separation of judiciary and executive, the rigour of organisation, its repression of human feelings and its use of military power...from Athens it acquired its desire for knowledge, its scientific quest, its pursuit of arts and its canons of criticisms.

Ashcroft (1999) supports this premise from a slightly different approach, whilst acknowledging the importance of universities' role in the policies of 'lifelong learning', Ashcroft (ibid) stresses that one of the most important functions of a university in a democracy is to take long term views that cross decades "...to question, challenge and so to protect democracy." Without this freedom to challenge ideas, and create new knowledge, universities, as well as the press and the judiciary, would not be able to support human rights, "it is no coincidence that when democratically elected politicians or their agencies attempt to impose authoritarian solutions, they or their spokespersons often lead verbal attacks on the views and motives of academics that question them" (Ashcroft, 1999, 1).

I would support Ashcroft's views and also agree with Duke (2002) that universities must maintain the democratic position to be able to provide for Newman's (1852) ideals but also 'learn to change' for the demands of this century. Duke (ibid, 41) sees universities as having three key aspects, which are 'teaching, research and community service'. Duke (ibid, 41) uses the 'metaphor of a learning paradigm' to show how different universities are opening up their access policies to students in different ways. For example, some institutions are continuing to follow traditional educational structures, whilst others are experimenting with specialisation in some subject areas, or involving other institutions in their provision (Duke, ibid, 41).

The traditional universities are acknowledged as being the ones that can trace their origins back hundreds of years. This 'educational dynasty' is, of course, connected to their value in the current 'market' in higher education (Williams, 1997; Ganobcsik-Williams, 2006). As this exclusivity becomes increasingly highly valued, the 'poly-technisation' of other HEIs means they have to defend the same cognitive skills values but also justify their place in terms of ensuring their graduates can also find employment if their courses combine other forms of knowledge or "skills and/or practical experience gained outside of the university" (Ainley, 1994, 137).

Widening participation has come, therefore, to represent the changing role of universities from being institutions open to a minority to a majority. The debate in the literature is frequently described as a transitional move to a 'mass higher education system' but Scott (1998, 169) used the terms 'fuzziness' and 'permeability' to depict how these developments in universities have progressed, arguing that it is the 'new universities' that have made the majority of the changes to their systems. This situation can be seen when examining how other countries' education systems worldwide grapple with the diverse demands of an evolved technological 'global society' that utilises all communication networks at its disposal (Crowther, 2004; Parry, 1995; Scott, 1998). Although the word 'change' is intricately linked to human development, because there have been so many different interested parties and demands placed on universities, it becomes synonymous with any aspect of educational provision.

Human Capital Theories and Social Capital Theories

Human capital theories developed in the 1960s from work of the agricultural economist, Theodore Schultz, who discussed the advantages in economic return made possible by educating agricultural workers in the production of their products (cited in Becker, 1992). Becker (1992) expanded on Schultz's work by applying his theories to all aspects of 'human' worth in a business context, explaining that in work related activities people cannot be separated from the 'knowledge' of that work. This he named 'human capital'. Rikowski (2001, 1) describes human capital in the same way in relation to education as the value of "labour power." Social capital theory, however, takes a more comprehensive and intrinsically subjective view of the common 'value' placed in terms of what is important to a given social group. So between any numbers of people concerned, this 'social value' will encompass what they trust in as their 'normative values' (Crowther, 2004, 1).

As economic competitiveness crosses the globe, the opposing views either clash or are ignored, in each of the 'worlds' in the different 'universes' of governments, educational institutions and businesses. The vast differences in the theoretical positions of human and social capital theories demonstrate the contentious nature of the discourse of successful economies. This is because the language of business has permeated the discourse and terms are used interchangeably with different inflexions, within the shifting positions of viewpoint and consequently, within different models. Thus, conflicting discourses exist on the meaning of collegial relationships; managerialist practices; vocationalism and what is defined as *professional*. The terms in the discourses are left undefined, used interchangeably and are often left open to interpretation (Edwards et al., 2002; Johnston, 1999). These academic models often use, what Gee and Lankshear (1995, 11) have identified as '...polarised and frequently switching positions' so although certain words are used by all positions (such as standards, consumers, quality economics, free-market and global) there is no consensus definition and explanation of the current view point on higher education's place in society (Gee and Lankshear, 1995; Green, 1997).

In summary, universities are in themselves "big businesses", striving to remain competitive they must maintain or improve their status, as shown by Brown et al, (2004, 218):

> The hierarchy of universities continues to be used as a key indicator of employability. It is assumed that the best graduates gravitate towards the elite universities. This view is actively promoted by leading universities as higher education has become a global business. The branding of universities and faculty members is integral to the organisation of academic enquiry. Claims to world-class standards depend on attracting 'the best' academics and forming alliances with elite universities elsewhere in the world, while recruiting the 'right' kinds of students. Universities play the same reputational games as companies, because it is a logical consequence of market competition.

The 'top' universities in England, often referred to as the 'Russell Group' remain in a strong position and aim to stay there (Brown et al, ibid). Other HEIs the post 1992 institutions in particular, must try to maintain or improve their standing in the competitive hierarchy. A key dilemma for these HEIs is how to admit more students with lower qualifications, but still maintain a high standard of education to remain competitive. Bauman (2001, 27) invites caution in relation to HEIs becoming slaves to a business-led agenda, explaining that "...in a fast moving society, skills become obsolete before they are fully absorbed". Regardless of their view of what a university is for, writers on developments in education generally agree that universities have to increasingly find ways to defend their position in the hierarchy of universities. This point is also raised by Beck et al., (1994) when they argued that 'risk' in a business sense in society has moved to one of 'risk in culture'. In other words, all education establishments have to cope with the 'risks' of their role. The lines of reasoning, however, are frequently not clearly demarcated. Gee and Lankshear (1995) have observed that it is possible to read arguments about market-based demands whilst employing supporting references to either traditional viewpoints or approaches. Other studies examine how the over concentration on the unstable nature of the market, and the dominance of human capital theories in policy decisions, negates the importance of the learning acquired in localised communities (Crowther, 2004).

Whilst governments' commitment to lifelong learning is seen by writers on widening participation as positive (Crowther, 2004; Parry et al., 2004; Tett, 2004) their main criticisms are based on the central premise that economic skills development does not give sufficient attention to the alienation effects of the policies. Too much emphasis on the application of human capital theories in the education system also does not allow for the uncertainties of the market. For example, 'employability' of students after a course of study also changes in the fluctuations of the market (Griffin, 1999), whereas, social capital theories focus more on the needs of the social context of the learner at the time (Crowther, 2004). As markets are never 'neutral' Crowther, (2000, 1) said that "…constructing the individual in cultural and ideological ways is part of a political project of fragmenting potential sites of collective opposition to structural inequalities" (Crowther, ibid). This situation manifests in what has been described as 'autonomy within inequality'. In other words, in the current system, some people will always have more 'market value' than others (Edwards et al., 2002). Ainley (1994, 135) develops this point by stressing that in traditional or "hard" (Becher, 1989) universities, such as Oxford and Cambridge, the views of higher education are still more valued in society for the "monastic nature of abstract and prepositional knowledge, as it is rare, like gold" (Ainley, ibid, 135). Writers on educational policy, however, disagree about whether explanations for higher education's changing role are theoretically structuralist or materialist, or post-structuralist (Ball, 1994). That is, whether or not the universities are part of the reasons for changing expectations, or changes in employment patterns dictate the need for universities' courses to relate more to employment patterns.

These issues, of course, are interwoven with different ideas about the practical and philosophical role of universities' purpose. The discourse of polarizing categories of elite/mass education, are therefore inevitably linked to questions of quality and standards versus academic freedom and government control. It is, of course, possible to argue alongside Scott (1998) and state that universities are unique organisations in any society. Their culture at times showing differential power relationships within a post-modernist framework or as a claim based on Foucauldian (Foucault, 1972) principles would assert, the universities' management structures both reflect and control the conceptual interpretation of such power differential discourses in university life. In other words, universities have always, and in their current form, will continue to have, a differential power relationship with society. Brown and Scase, (1994) and Ainley (1994) however, concentrate their arguments on the social inequalities still paramount in higher education, a view that is also stressed ten years later in relation to those participants from social and economic groups three to five (Archer et al., 2003)[2]. Research by Archer et al., (ibid) and Crowther (2004) for example, provide evidence to argue that debates about the success of widening participation are fundamentally flawed because entrance to universities is still socially selective. The students are starting universities with different levels of underpinning knowledge, so there is no 'level playing field'. They argue that both universities and students are caught up in the mixed messages of the debate surrounding widening participation. The government's 'broad brush' approach to higher educational planning seems to cloud the real issues beneath a good headline. For example, new courses are sometimes criticised as not being 'academically respectable,' as claimed by Ainley (1994: 134):

> Far from professionalising the proletariat, as the recent expansion of higher education pretends, the new learning policy in reality represents a proletarian-isation of the professions. It runs concurrent with rampant qualification inflation and the general devaluation through expansion of the major part of a more differentiated further and higher continuing education system.

Despite the strong differing arguments about universities' role in society, higher education institutions have always shared a unique relationship with those in power in a society at any given time in their history. For example, the main objectives of the early, traditional universities were training for the priesthood, latterly law and medicine (Duke, 1992; Robbins, 1980; Scott, 1998). In writing about the changing role of universities, it is possible to dismiss the importance of the fact that these early institutions were most protective of their 'knowledge' and certainly did not pursue the advancement of it for outside interests (Robbins, 1980). The language of widening participation is therefore a critical part of differing inter-pretations of what the future of universities should be in policies of lifelong learning.

Widening Participation as Lifelong Learning

Nicoll (2002) has noted how difficult it has been to translate widening access to education within policies of lifelong learning into practical proposals for development. This is because the meanings of lifelong learning are interpreted differently: for example, from a form of social control as suggested by Coffield (2000) and Crowther (2004); as a 'soft' policy objective by Field (2002) or a way of restructuring the state and its relationships with other public service providers (Edwards et al., 2002). Ranson's (1998, 267) work on what constitutes a learning society concentrates on the need for learning that is both 'social and political'. He argues that a learning society must develop within democratic principles to allow for 'citizens' panels to partake in the decision making process of developments for societies. Young (1998, 194), however, does not deny the importance of citizenship but argues that ideas about the learning society reflect real economic changes where viewpoints stem from ideas from three distinct models.

Firstly, he describes the 'schooling model', which encourages participation in post compulsory schooling, citing the Nordic countries and South East Asia as examples. Secondly, he cites the 'credentialist model' which given its Germanic origins, reflects how the Youth Training System in the UK in the 1980s had variable success (Parry, 2005; Unwin and Wellington, 2001). Thirdly, he refers to the 'access model', which he sees as involving learning outside schools, colleges and universities. This access model is similar to the learning in a 'social and community context', as discussed by Crowther (2004). Young (1998, 203) has stressed that none of these models adequately address society's learning needs and proposes an 'evaluative model' that "…starts with the recognition that all social life involves learning, whether conscious and planned or not". Again, this model shares similarities to Crowther's (2004) viewpoint.

Archer (2001) and Haggis (2001) both stress the importance of two other aspects of the nature of the discourse of widening participation. Firstly, they argue that the language used works on a premise that widening participation is 'positive' which is generally accepted in the literature but also notes that the professional literature can also be negative when it talks of 'social exclusion'. Secondly, they both highlight the need for caution when talking of 'widening participation' in terms of written qualifications. It is the requirement of competent levels of literacy necessary to partake in the educational provision of 'widening participation' that may be a further barrier to its further success.

Access for Whom?

In the writing on the intended participants of 'widening participation' in higher education, it is possible to identify four broad categories of potential learners who are discussed in the literature. The first group refers to the young students under the age of 21 years who may not have any previous family member who has attended universities. The second group concerns adults who are classed as belonging to social and economic group three to five (Archer et al., 2003). The third category refers to semi-professional adults who have no previous experience of a university education and the fourth category is a mixture of all three and refers to people who live in neighbourhoods classed as requiring 'renewal' (Reynolds, 2003). Regardless of the above classifications of the potential participant in higher education, a report on basic and key skills by Powell et al., (2003) showed how poor literacy and numeracy skills could prove an attitudinal barrier to widening participation. They stated that "...those with limited skills are more likely to end up in low or unskilled jobs, which are vulnerable to the modern economy, often leading to long-term periods of unemployment" (Basic Skills Agency[BSA]2001, quoted in Powell et al, 2003, 3). They also stressed the importance of the findings of the Moser Report (1999) which revealed that approximately 20 per cent of adults in England, about seven million people "have more or less severe problems with basic skills, in particular with what is generally called functional literacy and functional numeracy" (Powell et al., 2003, 6). They quoted further from the Moser Report (1999, ibid, 7) that "...it is staggering that over the years millions of children have been leaving school hardly able to read and write, and that today millions of adults have the same problem". A further report on the '14–19 Curriculum and Qualifications Reform' (Tomlinson, 2004) also recognised the need for further attention to the basic writing skills of students.

Whilst acknowledging the professional and formal networks required to help improve literacy and numeracy standards, Crowther (2000, 2) stresses the importance of appreciating the nature of the struggle of people living in poverty. He said "...the dominant discourse has difficulty in conceptualising non-participation as a form of resistance...if education is a good thing, why should it be resisted?" Crowther (ibid) argues that people resist for 'good reasons', pointing out the importance of two forms of resistance. Firstly, he identified 'frictional' resistance involving a struggle to escape from power that is not necessarily direct conflict.

Secondly, resistance can be viewed as a new base of power in itself, such as preference for learning in the community. Crowther (2004) further argues that not all people see the 'inclusive' approach in the professional literature in a positive light, suggesting a way around this is to redefine learning. Reynolds' (2003) research into neighbourhood renewal initiatives would also offer some support to Crowther's (2000, 2004) assertions. She stresses the critical nature of the work of multi-agencies to build confidence in these severely socially and economically disadvantaged areas before any of its members may be encouraged to consider a form of further or higher education. With the departments of Health, Social Services and Education, working alongside on programmes such as Sure Start (a multi-agency initiative working with families with children aged 0–4 years) sensitive data and information can be shared. Reynolds (2003) further argues for a new language for widening participation, preferring the term 'deepening participation', taking her reference from the second Fryer Report (1999, 10) which refers to both 'widening' and 'deepening' participation. In Archer's (2001) research into social exclusion, she argues that the discourse tends to "naturalise unjust practices, emphasising working class 'failure' while ignoring middle class self exclusions" (Archer, 2001, 3).

This key point concerning the issues surrounding negative labelling is further discussed by writers such as Armstrong (2000) who argued that the basic contradiction in lifelong learning is that inclusion is not the same as non-exclusion. This is because the problems of social exclusion are multiple and complex and affect both individuals and communities. Armstrong (2000, 1) drawing on the work of Bernstein, (1970) who said that "education cannot compensate for society" argues that there is no "ideological base to social integration". Poverty prevents people from partaking in education, so in disadvantaged areas the elimination of social exclusion is unachievable. Armstrong (2000, 1) further claimed that:

Seeking to promote social inclusion heightens awareness of difference and social exclusion. An example is the use of information technology to promote social inclusion. This leads to the exacerbation of the exclusion of those, who for one reason or another, do not access IT.

The competent use of Information Technology was one of the key skills emphasised in the Dearing Report (1997) for 'graduates' to ensure their skills are sufficient to find employment. Research into graduateness examines the nature of employers' demands for skilled graduates and how this translates to curriculum development in university courses (Field, 1999; Purcell et al., 2003; Young, 2009). Ensuring universities provide courses which seem to be addressing employers' needs is seen as a critical function of government policies for widening participation. Developing labour market economies can seem to be a 'middle line approach' between strong emphases on neo-liberal economic policies and social inclusion (Field, 1999). Tensions in the nature of employability, however, remain. Whilst there is still a general consensus on the required skills of graduates in the workplace, as noted in HEQC (1996) as: professional responsibility; teamwork; communication; problem solving; personal qualities, intellectual skills, the order of their importance and their relationship to other skills is debatable (Bell, 1996; Brown et al., 2004; Purcell et al., 2003).

An investigation by Purcell et al., (2003) examined how widening access to higher education had changed the nature of the type of work graduates were able to find. One of the key aspects of their findings was that there was a wage differential between younger and more mature graduates, suggesting further tensions in the different aspects of 'returning to education'.

Initiatives for widening participation in higher education, therefore, face a number of challenges. From how to attract learners into the higher education system, who previously have either not desired it, or have chosen different ways of living and working. To ensuring that the students the universities do enrol, are retained to completion on courses that are seen as 'competitive' in the working environment. In turn, the implications of widening participation present a range of challenges and these are discussed in the next chapter. These challenges are related to how the management of universities support students' learning in terms of the teaching of subjects.

Conclusion

This chapter has provided an overview of the complex nature of widening participation and I have argued that there has been an increase in access to universities, and that is to be welcomed. There has not, however, been a widening of participation. I started the chapter with the analytical metaphor of 'parallel universes' and have shown how policies, often well intentioned, have been self-contradictory. The different lines of argument have been running alongside but not communicating *across* or *within* each other, coinciding, but developing at different rates. In particular, this is shown in the discourse about successful claims of widening participation in higher education. Student numbers have undoubtedly increased, but the numbers of students seeking help with their writing skills has also increased. This offers evidence to suggest that one of the reasons students withdraw from their course is because they feel unable to cope with the demands of study at HE level. I have suggested in this chapter that students' levels of literacy have a direct effect on their intention and 'willingness' to participate in a higher education. This claim is further argued throughout the book, starting with a discussion of language and literacy in the next chapter. In chapter 3, I examine the tensions in the discourse of language and literacy and show how the different implications of the various meanings of the terms, become metaphorical wormholes (Chown, 2007) that become subjugated, lost between the spaces within the translations. I explain how the different 'worlds' in all the 'parallel universes' then manifest in the discourse of teaching and learning in higher education. The 'world' of teaching in higher education is so diverse and was the main area of conflict in the researched institution, so I have moved this topic to chapter 4.

Between the Text Comment

The literature review for the PhD thesis formed the main content of this chapter. It was collected over the 6 years of the formal data collection period and developed over the last 6 years. The long, lingering worrying question that stayed with me during this time was, why? Why were some universities becoming so 'anti-educational' when the overview of the extensive evidence highlighted here is so overwhelmingly pointing the other way? Perhaps it was just this university? I cannot answer it. The students attending the SSC were keen to find out how to understand their chosen subject. They wanted more help, not less, New World University was obsessed with self-support electronic systems that the students did not want and some could not even use. Who was making the decisions about the curriculum at NWU? I felt as if I was in a physical nightmare, haunted by a line from Kafka's (1963) novel, The Trial:

Who are these people? On what authority do they represent?

Where was the communication? I do not know. If the evidence provides an alternative argument(s) - why was it not considered? Do we just imagine that universities are *knowledge institutions* and *learning organisations*? Perhaps we do.

End of Comment

The formal writing style recommences with Chapter 3.

NOTES

[1] Sure Start is a multi-agency initiative working with families with children aged 0–4 years.
[2] Archer *et al* (2003) conducted a study exploring the educational experiences and constructions of HE among working class groups.

DEAR ALIEN - DO YOU SPEAK ENGLISH AS ONE OF YOUR LANGUAGES PLEASE?

INTRODUCTION

What's in a Word?

In the previous chapter, the main policy issues were described that have surrounded the initiatives to widen participation in higher education. The language of the policy discourse embraces all the different aspects of the worlds within worlds of the multiverse (Chown 2007) as depicted in Table 4, described in Chapter 2. In this chapter, the complex nature of language and literacy will be examined further. This will show how the language of business has permeated all aspects of universities' educational provision. This has resulted in the complexity of the 'skills' involved in developing language and literacy becoming lost within the 'dimensions of different influences' on the role and purpose of higher education. This in turn, has meant the nature of the difficulty of contextualising writing tasks is misunderstood. Hence, the paradoxical demands on SSCs can be demonstrated by reviewing how the different expectations of 'good writing' manifested in students' queries for help with their academic work. The chapter outlines the reasons for the choice of the theoretical framework for the formal study. This method formed a useful structure in which to explore the impact of the diverse language surrounding the issues of increased access to universities. This will show how the differentiated discourse resulted in such varied expectations of how SSC staff could offer students help with their studies. These differences result in opposing views of whether the role of SSCs is to *teach* or support students and are discussed in the following Chapter 4.

Section 1 A Theoretical Framework of Language and Literacy

In the first part of the section, I will explain the nature of the generic aspects of the issues of language and literacy that have affected widening participation in higher education. I will then draw on these comments to illustrate how this discourse subsequently raised problems in how the work of SSCs are conceptualised. The language used to describe all the different aspects of widening participation in higher education, results in a confused and contradictory discourse (Gee and Lankshear, 1995).

Within the 'world views' in the 'parallel universes', there are a number of different meanings employed in the use of the terms "access", "widening participation" and "literacy". In the formal research I chose a literacy framework based on a Foucauldian analysis to provide a structure through which to examine the different inferences

(Foucault, 1972) and I summarise how this was employed here. The discourse is exceedingly complex, and the methodological approach I employed, is just one of the many possible paths through the literature. I did consider taking one of the issues, for example, 'lifelong learning' and then exploring the surrounding nature of the associated meanings. I decided against this approach, in favour of the method chosen, because I wanted to stay focussed on the impact of the different meanings, on the work in SSCs. I realised if I chose as my standpoint, one topic in language and literacy, it may involve a necessary movement away from SSCs. I do, therefore, accept the criticism that this section of the book offers only a cursory acknowledgement of the complexity of language and linguistics in higher education. Other writers have provided a very thorough insight into these areas and provide much more comprehensive coverage than it is possible for me to do within the confinements of this text (see inter alia, Edwards and Nicoll, 2001; Fairclough, 2000b; Hyland, 2004; Rose, 2001). They have also drawn on the work of Foucault to examine the 'power-knowledge' in the 'political nature' of the use of the terms "access", "widening participation" and "literacy". Their post-structuralist readings of the discourse of these terms, appears within the literature in writing that is also frequently termed 'lifelong learning' they show how by omitting certain words in specific combinations they "exclude or displace other combinations" (Ball, 1994, 18). As argued by Ball (ibid, 18) "…we must make allowance for the complex and unstable process whereby discourse can be an instrument and an effect of power, but also a hindrance, a stumbling block, a point of resistance and a starting point for an opposing strategy".

My writing has been strongly influenced by these post-modernist/post-structuralist perspectives but during the course of conducting the quantitative part of the research into widening participation and the work of SSCs, I found that I had to make a decision from a specific standpoint; whilst the qualitative part allowed for the acknowledgement of issues across the field, the very nature of the quantitative enquiry, meant this was not possible. Otherwise I could not create the definitive boundaries of the variables and statistical instruments of measurement. This however, gave me a dilemma, if I set boundaries, I was not applying a post-structuralist approach, if I did not, and I could not create my quantitative variables or the statistical model.

So to resolve this dilemma, I split the claims made in the research. I wrote about the qualitative interpretations in a post-modernist style, but I acknowledged the problems by reference to the work of other theorists and these are discussed below. Post-modernist viewpoints across all disciplines challenge the notion that any method, theory, or discourse can have a universal superiority. Post-modernist views, therefore, both take place equally as literacy events within literacy practices. This means that any interpretation of meaning expressed in a written viewpoint is itself an example of an 'event', but it is written within the 'practice' of the theoretical perspective in which it is based. A further contention, in post-modernist views, however, is that the meaning of "literacy" itself is heavily contested and crosses all aspects of language and meaning (Ivanic, 1997; Lea and Steirer, 2000). Ivanic (ibid) explains that "literacy" when taken to mean reading and writing, within post-modernist discourse, is inseparable from its societal context, but that the interpretation of language is also highly personal when she argued that (ibid, 345) "writing is not a neutral 'skill' but a socio-political act of identification", originating from the writer's identity within any given context.

These different applications and interpretations of literacy and discourse are then, as I see it, at the heart of the theoretical weaknesses in strictly post-modernist viewpoints. Spiro's (1996) summary, however, allows for these flaws to be addressed somewhat when an explanation of the basic tenets of postmodernism are approached from both epistemological and ideological grounds. Spiro (ibid) argued that if the study of humans (anthropology) cannot be a science because it is based on subjectivity, it follows that people working in the sciences cannot therefore claim to have discovered objective truth; he suggested that since objectivity is an illusion, it cannot have supremacy over other ideological arguments. Language cannot be discussed or separated from all societies, because it is the crucial means of communication. It does not 'reflect' social reality but offers opportunities for the creation of different meanings.

During the course of creating the conceptual framework for the study, therefore, my thinking moved away from post-structuralism (Giddens and Turner, 1987). Whilst retaining the principles of a Foucauldian (1972) model, I realised that I was now working from within the context of conflict theorists; in particular, the work of Lather (1991). I do, therefore, share the view of Lather (1991) in stressing that setting up theoretical boundaries does not in any way detract from debating issues in a 'post-modernist' style. So this was the reason I chose quantitative methods to support the interpretative, qualitative research methods in the formal study. In fact, creating structural variables from chosen theories can, thereby, strengthen qualitative arguments.

Whilst post-modernism and post-struturalism provide mechanisms to challenge established discourse, which in this book, is the 'power-knowledge' of the differentiating discourse of widening participation in higher education; I acknowledge the contradictions and criticisms inherent in post-modernism. The decision was made, therefore, to refer to other models of research that are fundamentally post-modernist in approach, but also to draw on techniques that enable alternative interpretations and analysis. Two such studies are those of Lather (1991) and Haggis (2003). Lather's (1991) work was chosen because, although it is fundamentally post-modernist in its perspectives, it addresses issues of theoretical weaknesses by embracing the advantages of utilising both qualitative and quantitative research methodologies. The two key aspects of Lather's (1991; 1992 and 1993) research of particular interest to me, are: a) her work on literacy and language within education; and b) her research designs utilising statistical methods. The critical language studies in the educational research work of Lather (1991), whose theories were influenced by the work of Paulo Freire (1973), formed a guide on how to approach the complexities of the issues found in students' queries at the case study SSC. The study also draws on the educational research of student learning by Haggis (2001; 2003) because she examines the nature of students' experiences of learning. Haggis' (ibid) research also offered further insights into the dilemmas and contradictions inherent in the discourse of the policies of widening participation. In 2009, Haggis reviewed the literature on students learning in the mainstream education journals, she argued that educationists in the main educational journals do not seem to reference any of the findings of the very rich fields of study reported in sociolinguistics and developmental psychology (Haggis 2009). As the research into language and writing is therefore, not broadly embraced by other writers on widening participation and social policy, the opportunity to fully appreciate the dilemmas of supporting students learning is missed. I would argue that this is one of the reasons why SSCs are conceptualised as 'low skills work' (HERA, 2005) and subordinate to teaching on main stream courses. The discourse analysis as shown in the work of Richardson (2000), Ellis and Bochner, (2000) and other language and literacy theorists (see inter-alia Barton et al., 2000; Hyland, 2004; Lea and Street, 2000) provide ways of exploring the meanings of the writings on widening participation. The research evidence for this book can then be said to be located in the field of New Literacies (see for example, Barton, 1994; Barton et al., 2000; Ivanic, 1997; Lea and Stierer, 2000; Lillis, 2006), because it shows how an SSC is caught in the middle of what can be known as literacy events and literacy practices. A literacy event is individualised writing for a set purpose, or as Barton and Hamilton (1998:7) explain, "literacy has a role". These events are easy to witness, but literacy events take place within a context in which literacy practices are culturally based, offering different inflexions of meaning on value and relationships in a social context (Barton, 1994; Barton et al., 2000; Lea and Stierer, 2000). Be referring to these writers' work, it is possible to see how and why, the supporters of the 'low skill' (the literacy events) ideas gained favour but failed to appreciate the complexity involved in providing 'study skills support' (the literacy practices) in SSCs. Hamilton (1994:viii) explains this further: "literacy events are the particular activities where reading and writing have a role; literacy practices are the general cultural ways of using reading and writing which people draw upon in a literacy event".

Whilst I fully agree with the highly personal nature of perception in the interpretation of language and meaning, and I support Ivanic's (ibid) suggestions of the importance of the writer's identity in relation to language acquisition and writing practise; I believe that over the past decade, the further development of individualism and relativism within consumerist values, has added further complications to this relationship between the individual and a text, whether or not the text is read or written in a university setting. Fairclough (2000b, 164) provides an illustration of this complex new relationship. He shows that while the power relationship of universities to students has changed, universities, nevertheless, maintain their position. He describes this as follows:

Marketisation entails a shift in social relations and social identities which results in ambivalent and contradictory authority relations. The essential point is that once an institution begins to treat the people it provides services for in a market way, as consumers or clients to whom they are trying to sell 'products', then they acquire some authority – the authority which comes from the power to choose, and to shop around. How then does the institution maintain control over its own processes and procedures when it is trying to sell them to consumers in a market?

Fairclough (ibid, 165) further explains that universities are addressing this issue by the "redrawing of boundaries" between the institution and society to redress the "contradictions between regulating and selling" in universities. He supports this argument with references to the contextual differences in two prospectuses dating from 1967 and 1993 respectively. In the 1967 prospectus, there are a number of "obligational modalities which make the authority of the institution over the potential student quite explicit. For example, second year undergraduates are required to take…third year undergraduates must choose…" (Fairclough, ibid, 164). He contrasts this with the influence of the language of the market, which shows a move away from a text based style to a diagramatic style, punctuated with phrases and not full sentences, as shown in an example of a prospectus dated 1993. Its emphasis on the persuasion of the personal identity as in, "you take at least three of …", offers a further example of the influence of advertising style. Fairclough (ibid) argues that by avoiding obligatory statements, the university, however, finds a way around the dilemma of keeping authority without explicitly stating it. This change in emphasis in marketing style continued in the 2000s (Wilson, 2009).

These subtleties in language differentiation, although occurring over time, are then currently reflected in both the students' attitudes to their courses and how they view the writing help offered to them. I would also argue that, whilst students attending the SSC studied in the research wanted to 'choose' what they studied, they equally wanted to know what combination of modules/courses/and/or programmes would address their expectations and provide job currency to them in this same marketplace. So although they may be termed "clients" or "consumers" instead of students, they were aware, on a personal level, of the subtle power relationship of the university over them. The university may advertise and compete for students in the marketplace, but it still has the authority to award or not, the qualifications it offers.

In pursuit of qualifications, the students attended the SSC to try to find help or discover the "code" of writing in their discipline, and the intense, intricate relationships involved at each stage of the literacy and discourse development, is itself, inseparable from current societies' demands and influence. In writing up the research and this book, I would fully support the recommendation by Ivanic (1997, 109) when she argued that, "academic literacy is not a neutral, unproblematic skill which students simply have to acquire, but a multiple, complex and contested set of social practices which should be given more explicit and critical attention by all members of the academic community". I would also agree with her assertion of the importance of academic tutors providing the means to show students how to develop the "critical language awareness" through consciousness raising and that "learners need to be aware that writing is an extremely complex social act, and it is not their weakness which causes them to get stuck with it" (ibid, 339). By this, Ivanic (ibid) is suggesting that by raising awareness of the "critical" aspects of language usage in a given context, aspects of the students' anxieties of the appropriate style of writing, can be addressed. For example, this could be showing students how to present work, paraphrase technical references and write in the required style for case study reports.

In terms of existing critical language awareness, HEIs would argue they have done much to help support students who get "stuck" with their writing and their studies, both on course and, as in this research, through the additional support offered by centralised services, such as SSCs. I would however, further argue that the "situated and institutional literacies" (Barton et al., 2000) in the academic setting of an HEI, have also become more, not less, complex with the influence of the discourse and policies of marketisation. This has a two-fold effect. Firstly, lecturers have become more entrenched in how they view the importance of their role, the way they work and in how they advise students, nervously viewing the ability of SSCs to help "their students" in any more than a general way. Consequently, this materialises in how the subject tutors stress how they want students to write up their work. Secondly, students may have their own views on the personal struggle with the writing process, but equally, they want the 'best' of what the marketised system can offer them, the best "value for money", while they are on the degree course. So that while the tutors in the SSCs can help students with their studies and their course work, students also have a concern about the level of help given to them by SSC tutors. The students want reassurance that the help is 'good enough' for their course.

There is no commonly agreed discourse or 'literacy' across the disciplines (Gee, 2000). It follows; therefore, that lecturers from the various disciplines working in an SSC will have different views on what constitutes study skills and writing support and what is the *correct* academic style for written work at universities. It would, in my opinion, be a flaw of theories of literacy within post-modernism to suggest that the writer's identity would supersede the disciplinary differences in what constitutes *appropriate writing*. This is because the writing of a piece of work is only a part of the learning of the 'knowledge' of a subject area. Other parts of this knowledge are made up different attitudes to literature, research, study skills and application of learning that exist in the subject areas. The work of Becher (1989) and Becher and Trowler, (2001), therefore, provided a context for the issues raised in the research. They have shown how "…disciplinary classification is not cast in stone but is socially constituted" (Becher and Trowler, ibid, 59).

This means that Barton et al.'s (2000) "situated and institutional literacies" create a fourth dimension of meaning, *another world within a world of the parallel universe of the subject peculiar to the subject*. This specific meaning or 'writing code' if you prefer, therefore, is only understood by the members of that particular academic tribe (Becher and Trowler, 2001). It may be that although a post-structuralist (Richardson, 2000) interpretation may show how these shifting meanings in language are linked together to other aspects of social reality, the importance of the literacy practice in any 'subject event' may not be given the attention it should. Ironically, Richardson (2000, 923) alludes to this difficulty when writing about research findings, claiming that writing up research is not just the 'telling' of the work, the writing is also a 'method of inquiry' which is in itself a way of 'knowing, of discovery and analysis'; by this she is arguing that writers are not engaged in a static practice, language is not and can never be 'value free'.

In her writings on research, Lather (1991, 60) refers to the difficulties of ensuring 'meaning', arguing that the goal of emancipatory research is to encourage greater understanding of the issues that are found to be 'empirically grounded' both in the language used in the study and the issue itself. Lather (ibid) also examines further what Freire (1973) called "the culture of silence". By this, she means that the areas of language that are ignored, suppressed or oppressed are equally important as the established language or "discourse" of a community within any society. Her work, therefore, stands in the middle of:

> ...teleological assumptions of orthodox Marxism and the cynicism that characterizes a good deal of postmodernism. It is firmly grounded as well in a feminist appraisal of how power operates. Thus, feminist, neo-marxist, and post-modern theories and practices are blended together in a unique and insightful manner. (Apple, writing the Preface for Lather's book, 1991, xi)

Apple's summary of Lather's work shows the importance of her claims, as she is able to acknowledge the tensions in the meanings in the different 'definitions' of feminist, Marxist and post-modernist views, showing how they are at times, inseparable. These "tensions" are the "silences", where she refers back to the work of Freire (ibid). This, Lather (ibid) does by appreciating the essence of post-modernist thought, whilst at the same time, she also challenged many of its arguments in three main areas. One area of her research looks at resistance patterns in teaching and learning. A second part of her work examines the disparity in what it means to do 'empirical work in a post-positivist/post-modern era' (Lather, 1991, 1). A third part of her research involves evaluating how to 'write postmodern', which '...is to simultaneously use and call into question a discourse' whilst at the same time engaging in the 'struggle to find a way of communicating these deconstructive ideas so as to interrupt hegemonic relations and received notions of what our work is to be and do' (ibid, 1991, 1). I also found this to be true in my research into the role of the SSC. The findings proved the nature of the students' requests for help with their studies, but they were resisted (Lather, 1991) as they showed a disparity *grounded in the views* (Lather, 1991) of the role by management, the role analysts and some academic staff (Barkas, 2008). The impact of this resistance (Lather, 1991) was that in NWU, the contribution to knowledge, this research made, was therefore both "subjugated" (Foucault, 1980) and "silenced" (Freire, 1973). A practical demonstration of this may be illustrated by the stance of silence the managers at New World University made against the SSC coordinator's attempts to bring about curriculum change, whereby students learning needs could be met from within a course (Barkas, 2008).

As shown by Becher and Trowler (2001), the subject disciplines emphasise different aspects of writing practices. They argue that while there are agreed claims to similar knowledge domains by adjoining disciplinary groups, there are also three areas of boundaries where strong "territorial rights are enforced", concerning the "conceptual framework of the discipline, contrasts in style or emphasis, and the division of intellectual labour" (Becher and Trowler, ibid, 61). These territories are embodied in the study and writing practices of the disciplines. For example, they cite the following example:

> A physical chemist began by observing that the scientific background of physicists is based on deductive solutions whereas that of chemists is based

on induction. This distinction he suggested pervades the practice and marks the common boundaries of the two disciplines (Becher and Trowler, ibid).

Becher and Trowler (ibid) further demonstrate, for example, that the approach by biologists is different to the other scientific fields, as they take a phenomenological approach to their subjects rather than the inductive or deductive methods, more usually adopted in the sciences. The different disciplines' 'contrasts in writing style or emphasis', can be seen in the various ways academic tutors stress what they see, as an appropriate approach and/or writing style in an 'academic essay', as shown below:

the use of the personal to illustrate points (Social Anthropology)
the translation of the highly academic for the lay person's
understanding (Management Science)
a demonstration of reading and expression in own words (Social Policy)
the correct use of technical language and terminology (Biology)
the reading of 'technical' material and the information processing skills (Law)
location in historical context (History)
the use of good argument, premise, reasoning and conclusion (Politics)
the use of appropriate quotations (English)
the use of primary texts (English)
(adapted from Crème and Lea, 1997, 29–32)

The above illustration offers an example of how 'correctness' in approach and language is interpreted differently, so a student studying any two of the above subjects would be given conflicting instructions from their tutors on how best to conduct and write up their work. This situation is aggravated further in terms of appropriate study skills for each discipline as Becher and Trowler (2001, 71) explain. Subjects within disciplines place different emphases on how to approach the understanding of the topic. Some are theory based, technique or methods based and/or based on subject matter specialisms. They offer examples such as tax law within legal studies, crystallography, or Elizabethan theatre, whereby disciplines connected to different parts of the same topic favour one theory/method to another. Whilst a post-modernist perspective would doubt the reality of such boundaries, the position nevertheless remains that the student must manage their learning of the subject within the contrasting constraints of these different views.

In approaching issues involved in SSCs in higher education, Lather's (1991) work helps us to see how the complexities of language acquisition and usage are manifest in students' attitudes to study. Lather says that while language "frames; it brings into focus what goes un-remarked" (1991: xix). These 'hidden messages' are what Freire (1973) called the 'silences', the historical 'others', challenging our perceived meaning and understanding or what Foucault (1980) called the "subjugated knowledges". Although Foucault (1972; 1980) was reluctant to be called a 'post-modernist', his work on power and its shifting patterns is one of the foundations of post-modernism. His work is important to theories of post-modernism because it challenges established views of the chronology of history, stressing the hidden codes and assumptions "subjugated" within discourse and knowledge.

While the writers on literacy events and literacy practices, (see inter alia: Barton, 1994; Ivanic, 1997; Barton et al., 2000; Lea and Stierer, 2000), demonstrate the complexity of writing across the *parallel universes of higher education*. To stay with the literacy event, the SSC can be metaphorically captured as an *event horizon*. An event horizon is the point in a black hole where matter or light gets sucked in and can never come out again (Chown, 2007).

A Between the Text Comment – A Little Aside

As mentioned in the "between the text" about SSCs in the previous chapter, go there only if you are searching for the *black holes of skills*, but beware, you could be lost forever and besides, who would be the person with the appropriate "skills" to search for you? Mountain rescue would be out, not unless they have been sent to an SSC for skills training. Didn't anyone bother to tell you Linda, you are now expected to investigate other universes as we cannot decide on the nature of the known universe? This flutter of the mind brings to mind the Rumphold speech "the known knowns, the unknown knowns and the unknown unknowns". It's worth looking up; I should do that too, at some point, but not if I fall in the event horizon of the SSC. So, back to the "known universe" of the text, (yes but it's not really known is it, if a literacy event is as other writers also illustrate, the *worlds within universes* of the language of higher education, but we have to try to pin something down in the text or we would be talking in total abstract and floating around in zero gravity from here to eternity (and beyond).

Back to the Text

Haggis' work (2001; 2003) like Lather's studies (1991) shows how the complexity of students' learning, in the same way as the research into SSCs, is also frequently "subjugated" as it is overlooked in the vast literature, and particularly in the issues surrounding students' access to learning and widening participation. Haggis' (2003) research includes a study which explores the discourse of higher education. Haggis (ibid) examines how the *intended participants* of widening participation view further and higher education (intended participants are people on unemployment benefits or low incomes, classed as Social Groups 3–5). Haggis (ibid) argues that despite the multi-faceted aspects of learning (Lea and Stierer, 2000; Savin-Baden 2000) much policy literature and 'mainstream' learning and teaching theory still mainly focuses on the basic established models of deep and surface learning (for example, Prosser et al., 2003; Wilson, 2009; Wingate, 2007). Although these models are important, they are not the only critical factors of learning (Entwistle, 2000). Other factors surround language and literacy development and include students' level of confidence, motivation, their social background and the interweaving relationships with the individual and their social-cultural networks (Haggis, 2001, 2003; Haggis & Pouget 2002; Ivanic, 1997; Taylor et al., 1988). As educational policies are further directed to the non-traditional or regional student (Bowl, 2001), the 'certainties underpinning these views of learning are being challenged' (Haggis, 2003, 1).

Over two decades ago, Taylor et al (1988, 2) stressed the importance of the "close connection between the nature and quality of our students' language and the nature and quality of their learning". They found that the effects of home and personal circumstances and their own level of language skills had a direct input into how confident they felt about learning to study in any given context. If they lost confidence in identifying what was the *right language* to use in spoken and written work in an academic setting, they would leave the course. The nature of this personal language *code* was intensely evaluated by Bernstein's work in the 1970s, and the sensitive appreciation of which is just as important with current students over thirty years later (Bernstein, 2000).

The findings of the formal research conducted, and the continued work in SSCs in 2010, would support Bernstein's, (1970, 1977) and Taylor et al's (1988) research. Although students may be unwilling to articulate and/or confirm the above views, in the context of a confidential one-to-one tutorial in an SSC, (as in subject based, pastoral tutorials) students would often confide in the tutor, openly discussing quite personal issues; that is, if they were sufficiently confident and/or motivated to attend the SSC to request more help with their writing skills. In terms of the discourse of language and writing, Ivanic (1997) argues that the term discourse is used as shorthand for the complex concept of knowledge, of which language is only one part. Ivanic (ibid, 17) however, adds that "…as I understand it, discourse, as an abstract noun with no plural, means something like 'producing and receiving culturally recognized ideologically shaped representations of reality" the term refers to "a process" but also "a discourse". Foucault (1972) used the term *discourse(s)* in a wider sense to refer to the differentiated nature of those with more claims to *knowledge* in a given social reality. Ivanic (ibid) uses the term "identity" in both its uses as a noun and a verb. While the noun identity has the disadvantage of suggesting a fixed condition, the verb identify refers to a process. Ivanic (ibid:13) argues that identity is not socially determined but socially constructed, stressing that this involves struggle and saying that "…I would add that a corollary of power is struggle, Foucault warned against too deterministic a view of the effect of power on the subject". So people's use of language is, as Halliday (1978; 1994) said, a system of signs which convey meaning in different ways, Fairclough (1989, 1992, 1995, 2000a, 2000b) shows how power is enforced and reinforced in text in two ways – as social reality and social relations and social relations and social identities.

Literacy then, is often viewed as a skill to be learned and once acquired can be transferred to any context, but as Taylor et al., (1988, 2) have shown "…academic writing is not fundamentally a question of applying skills… rather it demands the creation of meaning and the expression of understanding". The meaning of literacy is also diverse. For some academics it means 'correctness,' whilst others are concerned with the student using the appropriate style and tone for a particular discipline (Ballard and Clanchy, 1994). As stated by Ballard and Clanchy (ibid, 19) "…literacy is not a uni-dimensional, constant capacity". The way to use language effectively varies from discipline to discipline. This means:-

> For the student new to a discipline, the task of learning the distinctive mode of analysis (achieving what we labelled cognitive competence) is indivisible

from the task of learning the language of the discipline (achieving linguistic competence). One area of development cannot proceed without the other. Language is neither simply the 'vehicle' for conveying the knowledge of the subject, nor is it the 'glass' through which knowledge is perceived. Rather language informs the knowledge; the knowledge finds its form and meaning within the language (Ballard and Clanchy, ibid, 19).

Ivanic (1997, 58) has also illustrated this in the following way:

> Literacy is both less and more than language. It is less, in the sense that language is a superordinate term, encompassing both spoken and written language, while literacy makes written language its focus. The word literacy is used in two different ways; meaning the ability to use written language. Literacy in this meaning has an opposite, illiteracy which is used by some to mean the inability to use written language literacy (ies) in sense b) reserving the word literacy for sense a) only mastery, or fluent control over a discourse.

The term "literacies", however, is also discussed by theorists from different perspectives to explain how power differentials in language are both generated and maintained. In any culture there are many different multi-literacies, which overlap, such as in Britain 'academic literacy', 'bureaucratic literacy', and 'literacies associated with work' (Street, 1994; Ivanic, 1997; Lillis, 2006).

Conclusion

Learning to read and write in the *culture* of a subject is therefore critical to students' progress on their courses. While most academic departments stress the importance of study skills and referencing, they do not however, generally teach how to know what to read and write about 'the knowledge' in their course, which is in effect, more important (Taylor, 1988, 64). The act of reading, however, is far from simple. The general assumption being that reading is a skill that is taught at an early age and practised. McCormick's (1994, 3) work examines the ideological significances of the task of reading, as she argued:

> It is, as Foucault and others have taught us, precisely in the details of this commonplace that the ideological glue of a culture is to be found. And yet despite the increasing emphasis on the reader's background, on varying contexts of reading, and on reading as a process, the 'commonsensical' objectivist model, which assumes that reading is a skill and that texts 'contain' information that skilled readers should simply take in and 'comprehend' correctly, still dominates much teaching and research.

McCormick (1994, 4) argues that there has been a reluctance to accept the complexity of the reading process because different disciplines do not appreciate the diversity of language and 'discourse', which is appropriate to a subject area. They are not, as she says, "reading each other". She supports the importance of seeing the interaction of the three different models of reading: cognitive, expressivist and social-cultural, stressing that in any one 'reading' one aspect may dominate interpretations of meaning over another.

In a similar way to McCormick, (ibid), Bock (1988, 36) also explains how university students have to integrate reading within these discourse/literacy practices in their learning, as they "subconsciously re-interpret language rules in terms of disciplinary content". She argues that these reinterpretations are accepted as the normal style as seen by the subject specialist who marks the work. The subtle nature, however, of how this process is "ingrained as general English and the correct use of common language, is difficult to pinpoint" (McCormick, ibid, 36). This aspect of the various nuances of writing in the disciplines becomes a critical point of difference when an examiner or supervisor from a different discipline or subject areas is brought in to assess a student's work. This example by Bock (1988, 36) of a postgraduate student working on a thesis in classical history provides a short illustration of this complex problem:

> The project was a source critical study, which proceeded by asking a series of systematic questions of each source in turn. The critical method was reflected directly in the discourse style of the thesis, where parts of the transitional passages were formulated as direct questions. The supervisor was not a historian, but a classicist from another speciality. He reacted at first very strongly against the style of the thesis, which he found aggressive and provocative towards him as a reader. He defended his perception with reference to the exclusively didactic-rhetorical function of questions in the literature of his own highly specialized field. In short, his long familiarity with this literature had led to a subconscious narrowing in his perception of the function of questions in writing. So, although his perception was based on the study of highly specialized literature, it was perceived to have universal application.

One of the tasks of lecturers working in an SSC is to help students respond to feedback from their tutors, so as the above examples show, in terms of helping students "decode" feedback from their tutors on their work which instructs them to *be more critical* it is not as straightforward as it may seem (Baynham, 2000; Hounsell, 1987; Hyland, 2004). A high percentage of the literature on learning and teaching in higher education concentrates on providing the circumstances for students to acquire the necessary autonomy in their learning, which is dictated by higher order understanding. What it fails to fully acknowledge is that on entry, the reading and writing skills of many students are not at a sufficient level to enable them to make the required adjustments in their learning style to function effectively as autonomous learners.

In the formal research study, the theoretical framework underpinned the choice of research methods and these are briefly reviewed the next chapter. In terms of gathering data, the process was further directed by Lather's (1991) post-modernist and post-structuralist model of what she terms Lyotard's (1984) "paralogic/neo-pragmatic validity". That is, the validity of scientific knowledge can be "...specified by answering the question how far have the goals been reached?" (Lather, 1993, 677). Haggis' (2009) study has shown that the findings from research into widening participation from specialist areas such as linguistics and psychology, is frequently overlooked by educationalists writing in the mainstream journals. This therefore, provides a possible reason for the lack of appreciation of the teaching function of the role of academic staff in SSCs, as shown by managers, personnel, role appraisal analysts and some academic staff in the researched university, New World University (NWU). The possible reasons why these misunderstandings perpetuate are discussed in the next chapter 4.

TO TEACH OR NOT TO TEACH? CAN YOU SPOT THE DIFFERENCE?

INTRODUCTION

The parallel universe of *teaching* contains a number of different "worlds of influence". They include different views of what is meant by skill, teaching and support. The five worlds of influence and the five dimensions, discussed in Chapter 2 and explored through the discourse in Chapter 3, all impact on the diverse expectations of what can be achieved by SSCs. These opposing beliefs result in the main mis-understanding surrounding the work of SSCs. The generalised belief that has become normalised is that the work is one of *supporting* but not *teaching* students. Each of the views from the various worlds presents a different interpretation of what goes on in SSCs. Although there are quite considerable differences, the central view is that only a support role can be provided in SSCs. While *guidance* may be given, it is claimed by those who misunderstand students' needs, nothing is "taught" (HERA, 2005). The difficulty with this assumption is therefore, clarifying the difference between support and teaching.

Support or Teaching?

Tait (2000) has suggested there are three broad categories of how student support may be defined. Firstly, as in the case of the work in the SSC support may be termed cognitive if it is aimed at helping students develop their own learning, secondly it may be termed affective when the support is concerned with providing a helpful learning environment, such as good lighting, plenty of space with accessible computers and so on, and thirdly, support can be systemic when it is related to effective adminis-tration systems, such as students have all the information they need on how to use the library, access emails and find the room their next lecture. In NWU, it seemed the personnel department, managers and some academic staff may consider the work of the SSC as providing a mixture of affective and systemic support rather than the actual cognitive support the academic staff in the SSC were undertaking in addressing students' requests for help.

In terms of the practical aspect of the communication between a tutor and a student, it could be argued that 'support' is a term that may be applied to confident students who do not have any specific learning needs, who understand what is required of them in terms of their subject, but are seeking 'guidance' on their work. The further difficulty then arises when this idea of 'support' breaks down when the 'guidance' necessitates 'teaching'. A 'teaching situation' starts the minute there is a dialogue between the tutor and the student (Ainley, 2000). The term 'tutorial support' is commonly used in higher education to refer to situations where a student or groups of students meet with their subject tutor (Booth 1997; Peelo, 1994). It is accepted that this is a 'teaching' situation, whereby there is an educational dialogue between the parties. For example, in a scenario where students in a philosophy class are asked to prepare their essay in reply to the question 'What did Aristotle mean by happiness?' they are advised to read specific texts from their reading list, prepare notes, send an email draft to the tutor for comments but most importantly, attend an individual tutorial at a prearranged time. In this illustration, the subject specialist, the tutor of philosophy, will provide both 'support' and 'guidance' on how the student may develop their answer but in order to do this, the tutor will have made notes either for their own personal record or provided annotation on the email draft. At what point the tutor chooses to 'teach' an aspect of philosophy, will depend on how the tutorial transpires. It may be that the student has totally misunderstood the question and the tutor must explain/teach what is required. Conversely, the student may have produced an excellent draft and thoroughly understands what is required but has in-depth questions about the specialist subject, so the subject tutor then 'teaches' and 'guides' the student to a greater and higher, level of understanding.

This sort of scenario takes place all the time in universities across all subjects and the situation in SSCs is not different. Students attend the SSC with questions about their work or the way they must proceed and the SSC tutor, from within their disciplinary background, offers the answers. The central issue here is that subjects are not homogenous fields; the knowledge in some subjects grows out of a trend towards specialisation of sectors, whereas the knowledge around other subjects increases through variation or diversification (Young and Muller, 2010, 7). Subjects also differ paradigmatically, for example, mathematics and the natural sciences are concept rich and have "hierarchies of abstraction" so if a student does not understand one step in the process, "conceptual learning stops" (Young and Muller 2010, 7). Knowledge fields in different subject areas change in other ways such as more knowledge of the past affects how the history of an event is understood whereas more understanding of space changes the conceptualisation of aspects of geography. In the area of practical jobs such as plumbing or cabinet making, new knowledge is 'crafted' and amalgamated into the vocation (Lum, 2004; Unwin, 2009). The emphasis on 'skill development' runs parallel to the mistrust in the validity of knowledge yet "we live in a medicalised world even as medical litigation rates grows exponentially" (Young and Muller 2010, 8). The devaluing of knowledge unless it has an immediate and obvious benefit in a given situation, appears to have grown in western democracies but is wholly absent in the emerging economies of South Korea, China and India (Young and Muller, 2010, 8). The disjointed discourse of skills and knowledge combine in a proliferation of the use of a "disabling and dehumanising discourse" that reflects a "peculiar notion that many occupations are either completely devoid or contain very little knowledge and technique and the workers doing the jobs are themselves equally deficit" (Unwin 2009, 1).

The discourse of knowledge and skills is where the complexity and contested values really collide and many questions are presented. For example, quite simply "what can staff in SSC actually do to help students if they are not allowed to teach? One of the major influences in the world over the past few decades has been the increase in the use of the internet and the increased availability of information has clouded the need for knowledge (Young, 2009). Many of today's students entering higher education have grown up using computers at school and college and have become a 'cut and paste' generation, where it is easy to find information and cut sections of it from the internet to make up assignments. They see no problem with this, as they are using references (Barkas, 2008; Lillis 2006). If a tutor then finds the section on the internet and accuses the student of plagiarism, the student is often perplexed as to why this could be an issue also, senior management are keen to keep students enrolled, so they are not always supportive of tutors bringing plagiarism cases to academic hearings (Williams and Carroll, 2009). Nevertheless, assignments or essays created this way; do not demonstrate the process of critical thinking that is required in a degree course of study. This issue is then magnified because many courses are assessed by course work and portfolios only, so that students have put together information without applying it to a critical or problem solving format. In the SSC, it was found that even very able and confident students, struggled with assignments when they were asked to create their own answers (Barkas, 2008).

To appreciate why universities' senior managers and some academic staff refuse to acknowledge the difficulties can be traced back to a 'knee jerk' reaction to early attempts in the late 1990s, to accept more students. The idea that a central service could support the needs of an increasing number of students, gained a hold in universities during this time when graduates having 'key skills' was the mantra of the day. Students new to higher education, responded to this 'mantra', and sought out the SSC, because they had nowhere else to go, not because it was the right place for them. In the researched university, academic tutors on mainstream subject courses, could not accept the complexity of the SSC, but thought nothing of referring their students to it, if they were either too busy, or at a loss as to how to help the student. During the course of the HERA role appraisal system at New World University (HERA 2005) I argued that it was the actual nature of the 'teaching role' that was the first principle in the flawed conception of SSCs. If students entering higher education were expected to have a minimum standard of qualification (Level 3, GCE A level or equivalent) surely they were ready to learn how to study in a university? Their needs could therefore, be 'supported' and 'guided' through the university's conventional subject tutorial system. What then was the purpose of SSCs? The answer at the time, was that SSCs existed to provide, optional, additional, study skills support and the senior managers and some academic staff in the researched institution, could reassure themselves that this was fair and reasonable, and never doubted that there could be any problems with this assumption. In fact, this assumption was so widespread SSCs blossomed all over the country (Thomas et al., 2003).

In another 'parallel universe' further education colleges had been providing a multitude of courses to help people either return to study or progress to degree level courses for over two decades, but the pressure on universities to widen access, meant that they accepted students straight onto degree courses, who would, before the Dearing Report (1997) have enrolled on an accredited 'Access to Higher Education course' in a college of further education. In the early 1980s 'access to further and higher education courses' (Parry, 1995) offered in Further Education Colleges, were the routes into either return to study courses or degrees in higher education. Further education colleges have extensive experience of providing additional support to students (Burke, 2002, Parry et al, 2004; Bathmaker and Avis, 2007) but universities have less experience, except in the nature of subject, and pastoral, tutorials. Further education colleges and universities, have a long and a complex history that embraces different philosophies about the approach to teaching. The methods in universities have generally developed from various theoretical approaches to teaching (Rowland 2003) whereas the teaching approach in further education colleges is a social practice model within an adult education context (Hunt 2004).

Establishing what and how to teach has always been a central focus of any university teaching. So over the past two decades, research into students' perceptions of learning and teaching has identified how and why they relate to their studies in particular ways and this knowledge has informed practice (see inter alia Marton et al 1997; Prosser and Trigwell, 1999; Ramsden, 1988). There has also been a growing resource in the field of 'how to teach in higher education'. This literature ranges from explanations of how to motivate large classes to addressing students' different learning approaches (Ballantyne et al, 1999; Gibbs, 1992; Ketteridge et al., 2002; Light and Cox, 2001,). Other areas of research focus on how students adapt to their studies, for example, Bowl, (2001); Knight and York (2003) and Kreber (2003). Despite this valuable literature, that contributes much to the development of the knowledge of teaching in higher education, there remains a lack of agreement over how 'learning' is achieved. At the moment, the central premise of a codified and agreed theory of 'learning' is not possible, as there is such extensive disagreement across the different fields of knowledge (Hager and Hodkinson, 2009). This means that the different interpretations of what and how learning is achieved in higher education results in the contradictory language (Barton et al., 2000) and differentiated discourse (Gee, 2000) as explained above. This situation is then further complicated because over the past decade, the emphasis in educational policy has shifted from the focus on the ideas of a knowledgeable and developing society as presented in The Learning Age (Blunkett, 1998) to a more directed policy strategy on encouraging participation from under-represented groups (Archer, Hutchings and Ross, 2003). Whilst these policies to widen participation in higher education are welcomed, the view that the proposed learner will then become motivated by a "choice" of routes into learning, is "constructed" on the idea of a "problem learner", that as argued by Archer et al (2003, 1) does not capture the complexity of the individual learning situations in a social context.

The different claims in the language of the government's policies and the stated aims, create a 'world of economic intention' (Brown and Hesketh, 2004) which then becomes a trajectory of dominating (Foucault, 1972) "constructed beliefs" (Bernstein,

2000) that are widely accepted, even though there is extensive empirical evidence to challenge them. This evidence comes from all the other 'worlds' in the 'parallel universes' of higher education. What then manifests is a four way dimensional split of beliefs across the 'worlds': language and literacy; knowledge; learning and teaching; and skills.

The 'dimensions' are not static and it is possible to observe very fluid boundaries, which only adds to the confusion of definition and application. Although the same words are used, such as *skills* and *learning*, the complexity and value of the actual physical and mental development of a skill is devalued and they are taken out of context (Unwin, 2004a; 2009). This dimension within the worlds of skills talks, particularly in higher education, is overtly simplistic, with its supporters refusing to acknowledge the complexity of the learning process in a given subject context, the actual content of the skill or how they are experienced for the individual (Ashworth and Greasley, 2009; Haggis, 2009; Standish; 2002; Wingate, 2007).

The different views of skills are reflected in different opinions about whether or not vocational and academic skills should be combined or segregated (Unwin, 2004; 2009) These different views are then intertwined with polemically opposing theories of how learning is achieved and whether or not the resulting skills and knowledge can be transferred to other contexts (Ashworth and Greasley, 2009). One of the impacts of this is the creation of the belief of the problem learner who needs skills to survive at any level in life. The belief in the problem learner is central to the dominant discourse of deficiency models of *skills development* (Hodgson and Spours, 1997; Hyland and Johnson, 1998; Wingate, 2007).

In 2010, many universities' courses have moved on from "bolt-on approaches" (Bennett et al., 2000) and embedded their interpretation of "study and employability skills" in the main stream subjects (Wingate 2007) but even these institutions may still hold on to centralised SSCs as a precaution, a safeguard to claim that general issues can be solved there, as demonstrated by other researchers (Thomas et al., 2003). In many of these institutions, however, a major distinction is possible to identify and that is, the centralised service for support in academic literacy is offered by professors in linguistics or other related subjects so ownership of management and decision making and subsequent respect for that process, is maintained through the discipline (Barkas, 2008). Whereas in similar institutions to NWU, the ownership of decision making and the importance of academic literacy as a research field in learning and teaching in higher education, becomes lost in the galaxy of different influences that arise from contradictory views of support, teaching, skills and how knowledge about these issues should be managed. This exceedingly complicated situation has a vast array of literature that each creates a world within a world, within a universe of beliefs, but it is possible to depict the issues as two, broad, albeit, huge, problem areas that arise in attempting to widen participation in universities. The first problem areas relates to how universities can change to meet the issues arising form widening access to higher education. The second problem area relates to how one of its solutions, SSCs, has to cope with the demand placed upon them.

The first problem has three overlapping categories as shown in Table 7 below:

Table 7. The first problem: Issues arising out of widening participation

Higher education as a 'world'	Issues in attempts to 'widen participation in HE'.	The changing student profile
Within it, are its own unique culture, views and rules.	Includes the three related aspects of society's development:	'Non-traditional students' who do not fit the model. These include:
A central view is that students fit a certain 'model'. They arrive 'fully formed' and prepared to live in this New Higher Education World of Learning.	Economic agendas which require more highly skilled employees. Education policies to ensure there are more graduates.	a) Mature professionals who have highly skilled training and expertise but no HE experience b) Young students with poor education attainment c) Young students with GCE A levels, who may or may not, be at their first choice university. d) Well qualified students who do not have adequate writing skills to cope with the demands of the HE learning environment
This model means that students can write in the disciplinary register and this is underpinned by their ability to know how to learn in Higher Education.	More graduates will mean that because they have the 'skills for the economy' they will be able to find work and more employed people will make for a happier more cohesive society.	

Source: Barkas (2008).

One of the solutions to this problem, as envisaged by universities' management, was to establish SSCs where all students could go to get help with their studies. The academic teaching staff could also direct their students to the SSC for help. This solution, however, presents a further set of three complex issues as depicted in Table 8:

Table 8. Solution to problem 1-presents another set of issues

Student skills centres (SSCs)	Academic staff in SSC	Students queries
Diversity of issues arising from attempting to meet the challenges presented by a multi-function cross institutional role	Academic staff have different views of what counts as 'academic literacy' in their subject and this varies in subjects within and across disciplines	Students' queries are a complex mixture of personal, writing and development needs

Source: Barkas (2008).

SSCs employ academic teaching staff and the solution to problem 1, then presents a second problem, as shown in Table 9:

Table 9. SSCs as 'the solution'

Management and academic staff see the SSC has having boundaries	*Tutors in SSCs do have to 'teach'*
Management and academic staff see the SSC has having boundaries and it must only 'support' but not 'teach' students. 'Teaching' is seen as the domain of the subject tutors on course programmes.	Students attending SSC come from the backgrounds as shown in Table 7 and have the needs as shown in Table 8, they want to be taught what to do, not told to go and find out themselves.

Source: Barkas (2008).

The move away from the centrality of "teaching in learning" is in part, illustrative of the trend to allow technological transformations in learning, such as online modules and packages, to be seen to be integrating with a re-conceptualisation of knowledge (Dewey, 1916).

A problem exists, however, in terms of what can be classified as a student support or a teaching presence, both in terms of how a teaching environment can be created and what is required for a teaching and learning situation to take place. The issue of whether or not teaching, rather than support was the essence of the work in SSCs proved to be an underlying topic of this research study. In a similar way, online learning faces the same set of questions about how students learn, as in the physical environment of SSCs: what do the students need and how can their needs be addressed?

In terms of online learning, Garrison et al., (2004:63), address this issue by deciding whether or not a teaching presence is possible to observe. This *presence* is made up of three components which together make up a 'community of inquiry framework'. These components are 'social', 'cognitive' and 'teaching'. In terms of online learning, the social environment means learners have to project them-selves electronically in what is often termed 'cyber space' as 'real people'; 'cognitive' means learners must be able to engage in a discourse in an electronic community and 'teaching' means that there must be some 'real person' who takes the role as a *teacher* providing facilitation and direction to ensure the other two components are possible.

Although online learning environments have grown immensely (Garrison et al., ibid) during the course of this research project, ironically, the students who attended the case study SSC, were frequently not that keen to learn how to study independently using the proliferation of online materials or online learning environments the university provides, but they did want to work with a tutor, in person. They wanted the reassurance of the *presence* of a person, not the electronic learning environment, regardless of how effective it was. SSCs, therefore, provide a physical teaching presence, offering the three components of a 'real social environment', the supported process of the 'cognitive development' of students and the 'creation and direction as provided by the teaching' as identified by Garrison et al., (ibid).

It is possible then to locate the teaching presence to within the cognitive model of support as explained by Tait (2000). Managers at NWU continue to view the SSC from a systemic service perspective so have no difficulty in dismissing the actual reality of the service because the value and content of the work in the SSC is incongruent with their value system (Winter 2009, 122). As suggested by Wingate (2007) any framework of learning has to be embodied in a subject specific context; but while it may be complicated and time consuming to examine ever subject and course in detail to see which methods/models are best suited to specific subjects, the complexity of SSCs have to be accepted, simply because they are part of the current process of 'learner support'. The value of the learning experience in SSCs has really nothing to do with what the tutor can or cannot do, or whether or not the experience is classified as 'supporting' or 'teaching'. As any teacher knows when the student understands and the tutorial goes well, its value is ineffable. As identified by Knight (1996:35) the idea that students can automatically self-direct their study is "misleading, independence is a goal, not a starting point".

The further reason management and some academic staff cannot accept the *teaching* aspect of the role of SSCs is because every aspect of higher education's identity is formed by individual subjects and disciplines (Becher and Trowler, 2001), so they are unwilling to see how it is possible for SSCs to offer a subject role, or even view academic literacy as a subject. Once again, another paradox is that universities offer sabbaticals to academic staff and Masters' courses to students to study the education dilemmas staff in SSCs experience on a daily basis, but they remain unconvinced that teaching adults academic literacy and that is, writing across and within the disciplines, is the main focus of the service that the cognitive modela of SSCs provide (Barkas, 2008).

This reluctance to acknowledge SSC's work arises from how academics measure their identity as shown by Becher and Trowler (ibid). Other researchers, such as Henkel (2000, 189) also found that academics define their role through their subject and this forms a "tangible social, as well as epistemological construct". This cultural identity is then reinforced by subject based national initiatives to support teaching, such as the Fund for the Development of Teaching (FDTL: in England), the Learning and Teaching Support Network (LTSN, UK wide) and the HEA. The irony here is that the SSC staff do work from the starting point of their discipline, and do not reduce their teaching to a generic competence, that Rowland (2003, 15) has said is unrepresentative of the role of teaching in higher education. He said that reducing teaching to a technical performance gives rise to two incorrect assumptions being made. These are, firstly, that "teaching and learning is primarily a practical, rather than a theoretical, activity" and secondly, that "teaching and learning are the special concerns of educationists and educational researchers who develop education theory" (Rowland, 2003, 15). The tutors who work in the SSC do teach students how to improve their basic literacy, but this is done in the context of assignments and within a task specific focus that is appropriate, as much as possible, to the academic writing style of the discipline. SSC staff are also in a learning situation themselves as they too, gain a greater insight in how writing within and across the disciplines varies.

Although tutors in the SSC do at times support students to help them become autonomous learners it is also a requirement of the role to teach students. Either how to develop their learning or writing in HE, or by teaching them an aspect of a subject or discipline. Management and staff must also acknowledge the point that skills deficit models (Hyland, 2004; Wingate, 2007), on which their theories of the role of SSCs are based, are largely outdated. Improving students' English or literacy in reading and writing is something that can only partially be achieved outside of the main subject area. It is during the course of helping students learn the 'academic literacy' of their chosen subject that tutors working in SSCs draw upon their own discipline specific knowledge (Hyland, 2004). They do not do this in isolation; they work alongside the subject course tutors, whereby each professional teacher hopes they can say or write something, that will help the student progress.

In these situations, it is not really possible to differentiate between levels of simplicity or complexity and/or allocate value in any particular aspect of a tutor's role in a given learning and teaching experience. Students implicitly understand that the SSC tutor may not have the disciplinary knowledge of their course tutor, but they value the professional help, none the less. The work done in SSCs is 'teaching' if universities' management or the HERA process want to classify it as 'supporting' or something else, it will not detract from the fact that a 'teaching and learning' situation has, nonetheless, taken place.

Conclusion

The attitudes of management, staff and students to the work of SSCs are further examples of the "silences" of literacy as discussed in the work on language by Freire, (1973) and Lather, (1991) that was presented in the previous Chapter 3. What is silent or left unspoken often "speaks" more of the issue at hand, rather than the dominant accepted discourse. While universities' management and academic staff welcome the role of SSCs, they see it as "bolting on" missing bits of generic skills onto students' curriculum, and not as important as the subject teaching. They are unwilling to accept that academic tutors in SSCs face the same and even more challenges, in helping students learn as main stream tutors. If confronted, the staff and students would not openly admit this view of the SSC, but their communications and their actions allows their "silences" to be tacitly understood (Freire, 1973). This book draws on the empirical evidence gained from the formal study, so the next Chapter 5 offers a summary of the research methods undertaken.

Between the Text Comment

I wondered why there was such a gulf of communicative distance between, what appeared to be, an increasing majority of staff at NWU and the SSC. As time moved on, I was reminded of Brown et al.,'s (2008) reference to "knowledge wars replacing bloody wars" as it seemed that even colleagues in closely related language fields appeared convinced that providing generic study skills was the sole purpose of the SSC. I thought about this and all I could think of was how strong the hold of genericism (Bernstein, 2000) had normalised thinking in NWU. I found this to be quite a disturbing situation. I considered that this dominant view at NWU had gained a stronghold in 3 major critical incidents in the history of the SSC. The first incident was the start of the SSC in 1999 (a pilot had run the previous year) when the focus of the role was on retention. The nature of how students could be *retained* by the SSC was not questioned. The second incident was the move of the SSC from the management structure of the education team to the library, yet part of the budget remained in the education section. The third incident was in 2004 when the managers and personnel's view of the low-skill nature of the work of the SSC was encapsulated in the role appraisal process (HERA, 2005). For the past 6 years I have been wrestling with the managers, academic staff and the personnel section of NWU to gain understanding and acceptance of students' learning needs. It seemed totally bizarre to me. This was an institution claiming it was a university offering "higher education" but some lecturers in parts of it, such as the SSC, who were advising students on their study, were *low-skilled* and *knowledge deficient*. My colleagues and I used to laugh about the irony of it all, but as this book has tried to trace how this view became so prevalent, the actuality of the issue was far removed from humour. You could imagine one of those satirical comedy sketches lampooning NWU couldn't you: "Yes, we are a university, but some of our staff whom we pay to help you, we have decided that they do not have much knowledge and are low-skilled. We have proper, knowledgeable staff but they don't think much of the SSC staff either, but we can offer you a good degree. Don't worry about the low-skilled staff, we don't."

Or is it just me? Have I merely imagined I teach? Have I only dreamt the years of study involved in the research into the students' request for help? Is all the evidence I have collected on different subjects and students' needs other people's fantasies too? Perhaps the quantitative data is just mathematical formulae?

There is much more research still to be done. Perhaps if I can encourage someone else to work with me, a group approach may have more success in persuading the non-believers that studying in higher education is complex process and certainly not without difficulties. Oh dear …it is a crazy situation don't you think?

End of Comment.

I return to the formal writing style in Chapter 5.

CHAPTER 5

A REVIEW OF THE RESEARCH METHODOLOGY
AND THE STUDY OF THE SSC

INTRODUCTION

This chapter will explain how the themes discussed in the book were discovered in the grounded theory approach taken to the research into students' requests for help at an SSC but in terms of the role of SSCs they are revealed most dominantly in two areas. Firstly, in the ethics of undergoing insider research and secondly, in the reasoning demonstrated in attitudes shown by the refusal to accept the SSC both as an academic, and a teaching role, which should be undertaken in a given subject.

The theoretical framework of language and literacy discussed in chapter 3 formed the structure from which the research methods were chosen. Before I could create the research design, however, the ethics underpinning the research had to be addressed. As this was an *insider* research project, the ethical issues were particularly important. Although I wanted to ensure I undertook a thorough, truthful and academically valid study, I was also aware that by doing so, I may encounter difficulties as I am employed by the university.

Conducting the research was a deeply, personal, experience. I know that effective research has to be objective and for it to have any validity, it must be authentic and as Denzin and Lincoln (2000) confirm, it must be *trustworthy*. I was most rigorous at all times when conducting my theoretical framework, methodology, data collection and analysis. As this was insider research examining the impact of policy in practice in a case study, I had extensive, sensitive, ethical issues to consider. It was, however, a totally all consuming project.

I organised the work of the SSC, on a counselling model (McNair, 1997), which was the most appropriate method at the time. This was to protect students' confidentiality and reassure them that they could have extra help with their studies without it affecting their entitlement to on-course help. I knew at the time, that this extra help was empirically problematic, as noted previously but I was employed to do the job. So while I can narrate the experience and research the issues, I still had to do the job I was paid to do. In terms of the research, I started the variables for the data analysis techniques for this research but also used them to help produce a simple descriptive report on usage of the SSC, for Senior Management, because the initial funding for the SSC was from external project monies, and auditable records were a necessary requisite.

The next part of the chapter will discuss the formal ethical dilemmas involved. I will then show how ethical considerations then impact on the reluctance to accept the academic and teaching function of the role. The final part of the chapter will then outline the research design.

Ethical Issues from the Qualitative Research Part of the Study

Ensuring that ethical research is conducted is a critical component of any study. 'Insider research' is particularly sensitive, so I maintained the anonymity of the organisation, staff and students by using pseudonyms. The research methods were all conducted in accordance with the British Sociological Association's Code of Ethics (BSA, 1973) and the British Educational Research Association's Revised Ethical Guidelines for Educational Research (BERA 2004). The substantial nature and complexity of the field of professional ethics has arisen from developments in many areas; for example, morality, philosophy, medicine, law, science and technology (Burgess, 1985). The problems of conducting 'ethical' research are intrinsically related to the relationship of the researcher with the researched and how this is subsequently reported; careful ethical decisions then govern what and how the findings are presented (Atkinson and Hammersley, 1995; Burgess, 1985, 1993; Fichter and Kolb, 1954; Hammersley, 2002). There is an inherent tension between deciding what is 'right' and/or appropriate in theory and practice, between practitioner and researcher loyalty and the institution/topic being researched (Hammersley, 2002).

Telling the truth, is the core, critical component of research, which Burgess (1993) describes the researcher's investigation as being either "open" or "closed", or "covert". In certain unique situations, such as in the research of crime, a covert approach may be justified, but the researchers in this situation will be governed by the ethical principles of the field of conduct as applied in the ethics of law enforcers and legal research. The British Code of Ethics (BSA, 1973) was set up to set boundaries to avoid the problems of research that is conducted in a closed or covert manner. Un-authorised closed or covert researchers are "seen as spies who violate the principle of informed consent, lie to their informants and deceive them, invade privacy, harm individuals both socially and psychologically and jeopardise the future of further research in the social sciences" (Burgess, 1985, 139).

I tried to conduct honest, open rather than covert research but acknowledge the difficulties involved. The ethics of confidential record keeping was challenged intensively for over a decade. As the institution was pressurised to produce auditable records, this filtered down to requests for data from me in terms of how the university was meeting its widening participation targets. Over the past decade, I had several disagreements with management over data protection issues. Increasing pressure has been placed upon me to produce more and more detailed analysis of the work of the SSC. Each request has been from various numbers of unrelated committees and reports for external funding organisations. While I respect the institution's right to data and to make these requests, I believe that there is a risk of students being identified and this therefore, could result in a breach of confidentiality under the principles of the Data Protection Act, 1998. For example, other groups working on retention or widening participation issues, have independently, requested detailed data on the usage of the SSC to track students. This I resisted after consulting with the university's Legal Representative, because it would be in breach of confidentiality and only outlining statistics by course and month have been produced. I was also concerned about the ethics of so many different reports being produced, especially when there was no interest in the actual content of the work undertaken by the SSC. This situation seemed totally surreal.

The ethics of managing the conflicting dilemmas of being a researcher and a teacher were also problematic, in physical, writing terms, as depicted by Ivanic (1997, 10) who writes about the role of the identity of the writer, in its broadest sense of meaning, to depict "the plurality, fluidity and complexity of the writer's own appreciation" of what goes to make them an individual. As discussed in the previous chapter, the ironies and paradoxes inherent in the role of an SSC tutor, in turn, reflects the contradictions in the literature about issues in literacy, post-modernism and what Gee (2000) has named "new capitalism". The next section discusses the ethics of the role of student support.

The data analysis in my research showed that the main query was related to writing skills. The lecturers in the SSC, generally, were confident to help with generic writing skills up to and including level 2 on the National Qualifications Framework (DfES/QCA, 2002) (equivalent to a GCSE A–C grade) but that any other help and support related to writing skills, was offered to the student, from within the SSC tutor's own experience and from their perspective of what is appropriate from their subject knowledge and/or discipline, or field. The fact that different researchers define the area of expertise of teachers in various terms, does not detract from the practical point; that the tutor in the SSC, offers advice on writing from how they view appropriate writing in their discipline. It is at this point that the work of the SSC is most vulnerable, because how can any one member of staff advise students from other areas? For example, students from 164 different courses visited the SSC during the academic year 2003–4. The answer to this, so far, has been that the tutors in the SSC, struggle with their own ethical dilemmas, and make their own mind up as to what, and how much, guidance is appropriate. They do, of course, encourage the students to go back to their tutor for clarification as much as possible.

Some academic tutors, particularly those who enjoy working in the SSC, claim to view the work in the SSC as an extension of their role in subject specific tutor support. In contrast, other tutors, including some who work in the SSC, see it as both a subordinate role in terms of their on course teaching, and/or as a form of demotion away from their specialist subject.

Since working in the SSC, I have however, encountered, both unintentional and intentional professional apartheid from my colleagues. I am no longer a welcome member of any recognised tribe in the university (Becher and Trowler, 2001). In my career, I have been recognised as an English Lecturer in one School and a Lecturer in Educational Studies in another. So now I am the SSC Coordinator, in the Library. I am regarded as someone to be distanced from. It is as if the employment experience I have gained before and during this role has somehow vanished. That is, until a course is under internal or external review, a senior member of staff wants help with their own academic work, study, publication, course design, review, or CV. They will then ask to see me in private, and very much "off the record". I know a request for help is coming when I receive an email or telephone call from someone, "who hasn't seen me for ages. We must get together to catch up. I miss you now you are not at our meetings". I do not doubt the friendship aspect is genuine, but the professional is not. "You're not going to note I came to see you are you?" They are careful not to put their requests in writing. The very fact that I am writing this book means that I am both a product of and a creator of the current process in the Higher Education system (Ivanic, 1997).

The majority of the students, like the staff, were lost in their own self-created worlds and they did not think too deeply about the issues they presented to the staff in the SSC. They saw the centre, simply as another 'helpful resource' and took advantage of its services, without stopping to question the qualifications or experience of the staff who worked in it. Other students attend the SSC begrudgingly and challenge you to help them, or attend "because their tutor told them to come. I don't want to come here, or see why I should!"

A student visiting the SSC for help, once asked me,

"Are you a proper lecturer?" At a loss as to how to respond, I paused, before I answered and replied,

"What do you think a 'proper lecturer' is?" The student responded with,

"You know, do you teach proper subjects and things" (Barkas, 2008, 123).

This question reflects the further paradoxes in the role of an SSC tutor. Regardless of the ethical issues, paradoxical and ironic, even though it is, the essence of SSCs' existence in universities, is because widening participation has opened up opportunities for students without formal qualifications, and many students, whether they are confident or not, simply like to talk to a tutor in person about their work.

The alienation of the role in the SSC, therefore, was a gradual process, starting with the dismissal by colleagues in the early study of the core teaching principle of the SSC. This opinion was then consolidated in the key skills meetings, where the lecturers argued that they already provided *key skills* within their own subject, which was further supported through departments' requests for data, so despite my defence of the role, the belief that the work in the SSC was of a non-academic nature started to take hold in 1998. Although I believe it is not possible to support a student attending the SSC for help, without creating a "teaching and learning environment" in one form or another, and secondly, I also believe that *confidential* means just that, and the students who think they are being offered confidential help should be assured that it is. Although the ethical dilemmas are interrelated, the paradoxes and ironies, however, are also related to how management, teaching staff and students view the service and the role.

Ethical issues connected to confidentiality also relate directly to the choice of research methods. In the operation and evaluation of the service, I adhere to the principles of the Data Protection Act (1998), so these principles had to be applied to the research methods. In conventional research into literacy and academic literacy, it would have been normal practise to undertake document and content analysis, but as the written work reviewed in the study was for examination purposes, this method could not be conducted, so the alternative statistical methods were employed as further discussed below.

Overview of the Research Methodology

In the formal study, two separate chapters were devoted to a discussion of the theoretical framework and methodological theories that underpinned the research

(Barkas, 2008). In Chapter 3, aspects of the conceptual framework have been discussed in reference to the discourse of language and literacy. Chapter 4 then explained
how this influenced the definitions of teaching and or support in SSCs. The methodology chosen for the study is explained below.

As outlined in chapter 3, the debates surrounding the issues in language and
literacy were examined to construct the two dimensional theoretical framework of
literacy within a post-modernist/post-structuralist perspective. The choice was then
made to create a study design employing both qualitative and quantitative then
research methods. The research study of the SSC became a little 'world within a
world' of the issues in teaching and learning in higher education.

In this study, the decision to use statistical measures was made after an interim
set of results showed how students' expectations of the tutor support offered were
beyond the generic remit of the SSC. For example, the nature and relationships
between and among the study skills requests, the profile of the students and just as
importantly, the identification of the boundaries of responsibility for the SSC tutors.
In particular, what and how much guidance was appropriate, particularly when the
student they were working with was not from their own discipline? As the students'
requests for help were wide ranging, a coding frame was used to separate out the
different aspects of students' requests. For example, 15 categories of requests for
writing help were identified ranging from improving reading and spelling to reports,
essays, case studies and dissertations. It was then decided to define the different
types of requests by making use of statistical models to help support the qualitative
interpretations of the data. The use of contingency tables allows for the evaluation
of the independence of a number of variables.

Combining Qualitative and Quantitative Methods

There are problems, however, when choosing a mixed model study design. This is
because the views of the acquisition of knowledge gained from each method
developed from competing paradigms, whereby it is "assumed that there is a
correspondence between epistemology, theory and method" and this is not the case
(Brannen, 1992, 3). Brannen (ibid) has argued that the research process is not unproblematic and said "in practice, it is unusual, for example, for epistemology or
theory to be the sole determinant of method". Nevertheless, it is often in the methods
of the research where the differences are most prominent. In the methods of data
collection in quantitative research there is generally a pre-set structure which consists
of a process of designing variables in order to test a hypothesis. Whereas qualitative
research is usually started from the opposite angle and the researcher sets a broad
boundary and then looks for themes, patterns and relationships (Hammersley, 1992).
In terms of data collection, the competing theories clash just as strongly. In quantitative research, the researcher attempts to remain as objective as possible and the
relationships observed in the data are examined through the application of statistical
models and/or tests, that are applied to the data sets. In contrast, in qualitative studies,
the researcher is often a participant observer and although subjectivity is addressed,
the interpretative potential in the arising data is seen as a valuable component of

the data collection. The main difference can be seen in the analytical approach, whereby quantitative data analysis is often associated with enumerative induction rather than the analytical approach more usually associated with qualitative data analysis (Brannen, 1992, 6). However, as Brannen (ibid) points out:

> the main methods of the natural sciences (which are assumed to be in the quantitative paradigm) are not synonymous with inferential statistics; rather they involve the process of analytic induction. In analytic induction, the researcher moves from the data through the formulation of hypothesis to their testing verification.

In other words, "enumerative and analytic induction have different starting points therefore: enumerative induction abstracts by generalising whereas analytic induction generalizes by abstracting" (Brannen, 1992, 6). Hammersley (1992, 40) also argues that the theoretical tensions that arise about the superiority of one method over another, have their origins in the last century when the issues of difference arose because of the dominant view at the time that scientific enquiry was more rigorously based because it employed the linear methods of analysis as is necessitated by quantitative methods. In more recent times, the challenge has moved to questioning whether or not any particular method has a "particular epistemological position" (Hammersley, ibid). The key differences could be seen to fall within the following seven categories:-

1. Qualitative versus quantitative data.
2. The investigation of natural versus artificial settings.
3. A focus on meanings rather than behaviour.
4. Adoption or rejection of natural science as a model.
5. An inductive versus a deductive approach.
6. The identification of cultural patterns as against seeking scientific laws.
7. Idealism versus realism (Hammersley, 1992:40).

Hammersley (ibid, 51) summarises the dilemmas each of these positions raise, by stating that "what is involved is not a simple contrast between two opposed standpoints, but a range of positions located on more than one dimension". He argues, for example, that the debate over epistemological differences is more of a "maze" than a fixed choice over "a left or right crossroads", either choice of method brings up issues and problems in the research study that must be addressed. In terms of paradigms, quantitative research methods are seen as positivistic as its origins are in the sciences where the statistical aspects of measurement and their direct relation- ships are the tools used in research. The development of the theories of qualitative research, however, has been concerned with capturing themes and description based on constructivist and interpretative theories.

The differences in meanings between the two theoretical approaches, however, are clearly compounded in the opposing discourse of the use of the term 'triangula- tion'. In the social sciences, triangulation is used as a metaphor in qualitative research to describe the technique of combining different methods to support arguments that a 'truth' in a situation has been found. Massey and Walford (1999) have argued that there is in an inherent difficulty in mixing techniques that are ontologically based on different theories of measurement and then claiming that this 'triangulation' proves something. This is because triangulation was originally a set technique used in quantitative research in land surveying, whereby fixed points in a triangle could be measured; the same results could be checked because the variables were fixed points (Clark, 1951, cited in Massey and Walford, ibid: 183). In the social sciences, the idea of using triangulation became popular as a research typology as a metaphor, such as: data, theoretical or methodological triangulation (Denzin, 1970). Massey and Walford (ibid, 184) however, argue that there can be conceptual flaws in using triangulation in this way. In this research, I avoided the use of the term *triangulation* in its postmodernist sense to mean a *metaphor*. I acknowledged the epistemological differences of quantitative and qualitative research and then approached the two data sets as distinct measurements or two different aspects of a social reality. To avoid accusations of creating one or more of the 7 errors above, noted by Massey and Walford (ibid), I did not attempt to make claims that the two different methods used in the study mean the same thing. I have, however, argued that because the *truth* (which is also the social reality in this case) is the same phenomena, which in this case, is that of writing skills, it was possible to draw compatible inferences from the interaction of the deductive and inductive logics of the inquiry. Whilst I would fully support Masssey and Walford's (ibid) arguments about the need for clarity of definition when mixing methods, especially when using the term triangulation, I would however, also agree with Bryman (1992) when he argued that if the different methods are used correctly, the two methods can support the research findings.

In summary, it is possible to argue, that there is much to be gained by combining research methods or alternatively, stating that if precision is required, a statistical approach within a quantitative methodology may be more practical, with more possibilities for description available within a qualitative approach (Brannen, 1992; Hammersley, 1992). The next section outlines the research design and starts with an explanation of why I chose a case study for this research.

Case studies are frequently used in qualitative research but they are not a "methodological choice but a choice of what is to be studied" (Stake, 2000, 435). A 'case' in a study can equally be an incident, person, institution or policy (Merriam, 1988; Anderson and Arsenault, 1998). For this research design, I have been influenced by three case study theorists. The work by Stake (1996; 2000) directed the physical structure of the research design methods. The creation of data analysis methods and techniques and their subsequent interpretation, was then guided by the theories of Everitt (1977) and Yin (1994). In the overall case study process, I have also been influenced by Stake's (1996, 223) use of the term 'persuasion' rather than 'model'. This is because aspects of the study did not adhere to any one specific definition of a 'case study'.

I have been "persuaded" by Stake's (ibid) explanation of the overall description of an 'instrumental' case study to describe the research into the SSC, rather than adhering to a prescribed model. This is because the SSC provides both 'intrinsic' and 'instrumental' evidence that has both specific and general applicability. For example, in terms of proficiency in writing skills, the students attending the SSC in the study, have their own intrinsic issues within literacy, the culmination of which, may also offer instrumental and collective insights into the issues presented by other students in other universities with a similar population. The role of the SSC has 'intrinsic value' to the researched university, but also 'instrumental value' in developing knowledge about the impact of widening participation policies.

In terms of data collection and analysis, Yin (1994, 13) claims "multiple sources of evidence show the convergence of the boundaries between phenomena and content". Analytical induction, as defined by Mitchell's (1984) use of the term 'case study', was applied during the interpretation of the issues raised from the interaction process in the teaching role with the students in the SSC. This means that the interpretations allowed for the identification of the questions to be asked in relation to the development of a students' skills centre in universities, rather than the proposal of theoretical generalisations. This is, from a qualitative perspective, the development of 'grounded theory' (Glaser and Strauss, 1967). The contrasting enumerative induction of the statistical part of the study was therefore, an attempt at addressing issues of bias.

The research, therefore, may be described as an "intrinsic-instrumental" case study utilising a grounded theory approach (Glaser and Strauss, 1967). It can also be termed an "exploratory" case study, taking a different term for the same purpose, but as further defined by Yin (1994).

The interpretative strategy of a general grounded theory methodology means that the theories examined developed from the issues discovered or 'grounded' in the data. In this study, the influences on educational change and theories of learning and teaching emerged from the issues as they were identified.

The methodological approach adopted in the study therefore, was structured from the theoretical framework, and the mixed model approach was designed to address the limits of subjectivity which are inherent in the interpretation of postmodernist and poststructuralist models. Lather (1993) emphasises the importance of what Lyotard (1984) termed 'paralogic/neo-pragmatic validity'. That is, the validity of scientific knowledge can be "...specified by answering the question, how far have the goals been reached?" (Lather, 1993:677). The mixed research design using inferential statistics was thus an attempt at addressing the possibility of bias in the research by using an experimental model to balance the subjectivity of interpretation. The data was also analysed separately to avoid the possibility of errors as defined by Massey and Walford (1999).

The early start-up of the SSC was made without any thought being given to the content of the *help* such a service could provide. Before I was employed, the rationale of the case study SSC was to offer students the opportunity for optional, additional support with all aspects of students' skills. It was set up without any policies and/or procedures and staffed by academic lecturers who were coordinated and managed by the researcher. The management of the University were keen to ensure the SSC was not seen wholly as a remedial service and envisaged no challenges in sending any student to the SSC.

In practice, students and staff as students, from all levels of undergraduate and postgraduate programmes, with a multitude of complex needs, have made use of the SSC's services. Since the start of the evaluation of the service in 1998, the pilot, the formal research period and from 2000 to 2004, with further analysis of the students' enquires from 2004 to 2009, the SSC has seen its cultural remit change and students often attended the centre, claiming their tutor 'told them to come', when their query is directly related to their course in a specific way and specialist subject or course knowledge is required to answer it. This illustration is an example of the major ethical dilemma of SSCs and that is how to address the question "what exactly is their remit?"

The SSC was located in the Learning Resource Centre (renamed The Library in 2009). There is, however, a certain irony in the situation. I had previously worked in a teaching team, but was moved to the LRC in the middle of the research study in 2002 (See Table 10 below).

Table 10. Timeline of the SSC's development

1997	Pilot of SSC located in Learning Resource Centre (LRC). Member of Staff remained in their School
1998	I was appointed as full-time SSC Coordinator. My role was managed through a central Staff Development Unit which had responsibilities for University wide Learning and Teaching initiatives. The SSC service remained located in the LRC.
2002	Management reorganisation – role of SSC Coordinator moved to LRC Academic Subject Information Teams. The location of the SSC remains in the LRC.
2005	SSC Steering Group started
2008	SSC Steering Group abandoned

Source: Barkas (2008).

The research was conducted in a post-1992 university, referred to here as New World University (NWU). It was previously a polytechnic until the Further and Higher Education Reform Act of 1992. NWU is located in the North East of England where there are five universities and seventeen further education colleges with a direct or franchised higher education provision. During the academic year 2003–04, there were 20,335 students enrolled at the researched university, including 501 enrolled on further education programmes. Of this number, 9,357 were full time students (Higher Education Funding Council, [HEFCE], December 2004). The NWU's standard entry requirements are a minimum of 20 tariff points from Key Skills at Level 3. Some courses specify grades in specific subjects and these are detailed in the university handbook and internet website.

The Research Design

The research was a longitudinal study conducted over eleven years. The formal research was conducted in four stages: a pilot over 1 year, two phases over 6 years, and the informal research continued for a further 6 years from 2004 to 2010. I utilised a case study design and combined both qualitative and quantitative research methods.

The hypothesis and research questions were, as Glaser and Strauss (1967) have shown, 'grounded in' the research topic and developed from the interrogation of the data. These considerations led me to decide that a case study approach would enable me to explore my research questions. The empirical evidence for the book, focuses, therefore, on both the formal and informal research periods.

The formal research aimed to examine the nature of the increase in students' requests for help with their writing and study skills. In order to do this, a literature review and a case study were conducted. To examine this increase the following questions were asked:

1. What is the rationale for expanding access to HE?
2. What are the implications for the concept of a 'higher education'?
3. What is the literacy level/standard expected in HE?
4. Do students understand the level/standard of writing in HE?
5. Do levels of literacy and notions of standards differ across the disciplines?
6. Can students be supported to achieve the level of literacy required?

The aim of the case study was to gather empirical evidence to address the research questions and subsequently examine the role of a Students' Skills Centre (SSC) in higher education in relation to the development of students' academic literacy. The research data was collected in three phases. The first phase of the research was conducted from 1998 to 2000 and was focussed on identifying students' needs. This phase culminated in the creation of a website for the SSC. The second phase was for a further two years from 2000 to 2002 and examined the learning and teaching issues that arose. The issues that manifested in the first two generic phases were then applied to examining the level of writing of first year students' onto a Law course, during the academic year 2003 to 2004.

The empirical evidence for the research was obtained by the analysis of five qualitative sources, supported by the application of a statistical model to the data evaluated through a five-way contingency table. The qualitative sources were as follows:

1) Learning teaching issues that arose during 7940 teaching hours
2) Attendance records
3) Questionnaires
4) Follow-up interviews
5) Study Skills Consultation Record sheets

The first part of the analysis was the application of a grounded theory approach (Glaser and Strauss, 1967) to the discovery and investigation into the literacy, learning and teaching issues as provided by the contact by the writer with the students during 7940 hours over the six years of the total formal, research period from 1998 to 2004. Further contributions from the views of the Lecturers from the Schools working in the Centre over the period of the research were also obtained during the course of informal and formal reviews and team meetings. The issues discovered were then further examined through questionnaires and follow-up interviews. The issues were fundamentally related to literacy and the quantity and type of help that students could receive from the SSC. As noted above, in the section on ethics, it was not possible to undertake content analysis on students' work which was to be submitted for examination, so an alternative research tool was chosen and this was the application of a framework for language proficiency.

The "Pathways to Proficiency. The Alignment of Language Proficiency Scales for assessing competence in English Language" published by the DfES and The QCA (2002) was the scale chosen, because it provided the necessary descriptors for different levels of proficiency. The maps provided a means of ascertaining students' proficiency in writing. Students attending the SSC, many without formal qualifications, experienced a number of problems trying to improve their levels of reading and writing at the university. This was because they presented pieces of work at the Students' Skills Centre that was level 2 or below, whereas proficiency level 3 is necessary if students are to be able to cope with the level of competence required in reading and writing in the first year at university (See Table 11 below. GCE A levels are at level 3, GCSE grades A–C at level 2 and GCSE grades D-G at level 1). Table 11 below shows how the mapping of different language assessment is shown across the six assessment scales for English Language and English as a Second Language (DfES and QCA, 2002).

Table 11. Mapping different language assessment scales

QCA				Council of Europe framework	National language standards
National qualifications framework	National standards for adult literacy	Key skills	National curriculum	Council of Europe framework	National language standards
Level 5		Level 5	8 ↑	(C2.2)	
Level 4[1]		Level 4	National curriculum levels	C2 Mastery	Level 5
Level 3		Level 3		C1 Operational Proficiency	Level 4
Level 2	Level 2	Level 2		B2 Vantage	Level 3
Level 1	Level 1	Level 1	2	B1 Threshold	Level 2
Entry level	Entry level 3		↓	A2 Wayside	Level 1
Entry level	Entry level 2			A1 Breakthrough	(Entry)
Entry level	Entry level 1		Level 1 Secure/Threshold	A1 Breakthrough	(Entry)
Pre-entry			EAL Step 2		
Pre-entry			EAL Step 1		

Source: DfES/QCA 2002 cited in Barkas (2008).

In the national qualifications framework, levels 4 and 5 represent higher-level qualifications, GCE A levels are at level 3, GCSE grades A–C at level 2 and GCSE grades D–G at level 1. In terms of the National Curriculum, English in schools is also shown as English as an Additional Language (EAL). In terms of English as a second or foreign language, the Council of Europe, Common European Framework of Reference for Languages, Cambridge University Press, (2001, cited in DfES/QCA, 2002:5), shows descriptors of six levels of foreign language proficiency offered as international standards.

The aim of the survey as a research instrument was to find out students' views. In Phase 1, the survey attempted to ascertain their expectations for the services of an SSC, and in Phase 2 the questionnaire was designed to ask their views of their study and writing skills and in Phase 3, the questionnaire was designed to ascertain First Year Law students' views of their writing skills.

The research literature on surveys highlights the difficulties involved in wording questionnaires to try to obtain 'truthful answers' (Cohen and Manion, 1994). The study of the use of quantitative methods in mixed design research helped in the creation of the questionnaires because it was necessary to define clear and unambiguous variables with defined parameters of measurement; before the data base could be designed. This process ensured that the writing of the questions was drafted and tightly worded to ensure clear questions were asked that were unambiguous, using closed questions, but with spaces for open responses. The use of quantitative methods also ensured that the coding of the responses for qualitative analysis was in accordance with the variables chosen for the database. Pilot questions were given to a random 10 students who attended the SSC to test the suitability of the draft questions before the final version was printed.

Students were then interviewed. As a specific research technique, Cohen and Manion (1994, 272) define interviews as serving three main purposes: obtaining information relating directly to the research question(s); testing or creating hypotheses; or providing an additional means of research evidence. These three purposes were addressed in the research. The interviews were semi-structured, recorded and transcribed. The interviews ranged from 20–25 minutes duration. The questions were designed after an analysis of the issues as they were presented in over 7940 teaching hours and subsequently divided into 8 sections as shown in Table No. 12:

Table 12. The 8 sections of the interview questions

Section	Title
1	The profile details: Gender, Age, Course of Study & School
2	General aspects of studying at the University
3	Course
4	Study Skills Development
5	Yearly Progress
6	Using the Student Skills Centre
7	Future Courses/Career
8	Any advice to potential students?

Source: Barkas (2008).

The total number of responses from the questionnaires to agree for an interview was 35. From this response 35 agreed and were offered a confidential interview, with 12 students turning up at the appointed time. The other 23 did not turn up after a second written request. Although too small a sample to offer generalised interpretations, the interviews did offer an opportunity for further insight into the students' views of their own progress in study skills development.

An interim set of results[2] from the qualitative part of the research, however, showed how students' expectations of the tutor support offered were beyond the generic remit of the SSC. For example, the nature and relationships between and among the study skills requests, the profile of the students and just as importantly, the identification of the boundaries of responsibility for the SSC tutors. In particular, what and how much guidance was appropriate, particularly when the student they were working with was not from their own discipline? As the students' requests for help were wide ranging, a coding frame was used to separate out the different aspects of students' requests. For example, 15 categories of requests for writing help were identified ranging from improving reading and spelling to reports, essays, case studies and dissertations. It was then decided to define the different types of requests by making use of statistical models to help support the qualitative interpretations of the data. The use of contingency tables allows for the evaluation of the independence of a number of variables.

The students wanted extended, task specific help with their work, particularly writing skills. This issue, therefore, meant that the SSC had to look for ways to clarify its role. It was not practical or appropriate within the guidelines of the Data Protection Act (1998) to photocopy students' work to form a literacy, discourse and content analysis, so one of the other ways it was possible to start to clarify the SSC's role was to examine the literacy and learning and teaching issues discovered. So it was decided to define the different types of requests by making use of statistical models to help support the qualitative interpretations of the data.

The statistical information was gathered from five variables noted as: 'gender', 'age', 'course', 'school', 'query'. The variables then formed the basis of the contingency table for the quantitative analysis. Quantitative research methods employ the use of numerical methods such as statistics and mathematical modelling and have their origins in the natural sciences. Within the social sciences, the terms quantitative and qualitative data are used interchangeably. For many researchers, the term 'qualitative data' is taken to mean the use of interpretative methodologies and research methods. For example, data derived from interviews is evaluated through interpretative techniques rather than statistical models. In contrast, quantitative data is the analysis of research through the use of statistical measures. In statistics, however, the terms are frequently used differently (Everitt, 1977; Upton, 1978; Wright, 2002). For example, Goodman (1970) defined 'qualitative data' as nominal and ordinal data, stressing that this data was the examination of the distance between points. These are also often called quantitative data. Interval and ratio data are types of quantitative data. Nominal and ordinal data are qualitative (Wright, 2002:8). In this study, the term 'qualitative' is used to refer both to the interpretative data, but also to the qualitative perspective in statistics as illustrated by Goodman (1970).

Contingency tables are a way of summarizing data by means of classifications within a population.

The mixed model design allowed for a thorough analysis of the empirical evidence. The combination of two different approaches also provided a practical example of the issues involved when writing about a subject utilising different perspectives. This was particularly evident when writing about the statistics as the approach to explanatory writing must be seen to be as objective as possible, whereas when I was writing the qualitative part of the research I attempted to choose words that reflected and developed meaning, rather than just allowing the findings from the statistical test to provide the factual evidence. This process would therefore, be an example of convergent validity as explained by Lather (1991). The next chapter 6 provides a summary of the results from the formal study.

NOTES

[1] The National Qualifications framework was revised on 1 September 2004. The main change is that the NQF now has nine levels (entry to level 8). Entry levels 1–3 have not changed, levels 4 and 5 have been divided into more precise levels – levels 4 to 8.

[2] Statistics prepared for the first annual report in the academic year 1998–1999.

IS THERE A LIFE FORM WE RECOGNISE IN SSCs?

The empirical research for the book was collected by both qualitative and quantitative methods as explained in Chapter 5. The evaluations of the early development of the SSC and the findings from the subsequent, formal research period (Barkas, 2008), were, therefore, extensive. I have drawn heavily on the existing text from the original study in this chapter but because the data collection was comprehensive and detailed, I have summarised sections to highlight the main findings, so for the purpose of illustration, I have chosen just one or two examples from each section to explain the issues discovered. I have therefore, divided the chapter into four sections. The first section explains the background to the research design and gives a summary of the key qualitative findings, the second section then gives an outline of the quantitative findings, the third section provides the summary of the short, applied, case study on first year students and the summary of the research findings then concludes the chapter.

Section 1 of 4: Framework of the Analysis

The framework of the analysis of the data from 1998 to 2004 was undertaken in two parts. The first part of the analysis was the application of a grounded theory approach (Glaser and Strauss, 1967; Strauss and Corbin, 1990) to the discovery and investigation into the learning and teaching issues, as provided by the contact with the students for over 7940 hours over the six years of the formal research period from 1998 to 2004. The issues discovered were further explored through the literature review, and subsequently examined in the second part, in the statistical analysis. Student viewpoints were sought through the issue of questionnaires and follow-up interviews. The findings from the generic study were then further tested against applied research into the writing skills of a group of first year students on a Law course in 2004. Further comments also include reference to data collected from the post-formal phase from 2004 to 2009.

As New World University's senior management wanted auditable figures, manual records were maintained for the academic year 1998 to 1999, because during the first year of operation, it was not possible to design a database. This was for a number of reasons. The first one was because the Students' Skills Centre (SSC) was set up as an informal project to support students' general study skills. No specific objectives above this aim could be set, until the extent of the students' requirements were known. The second reason was because the Centre was so heavily used, there was no possibility of allowing time for evaluation until the year-end report. This report, however, allowed for the identification of possible variables for statistical analysis. During the first year of operation 979 students made 1046 visits to the SSC. A statistical data base was then designed and set up from 1999 to 2002, when the records of 3420 students were analysed. For the statistical data, the queries were combined (Barkas, 2008) as shown in Table 13 as follows:-

Table 13 – Query types

Group 1 Writing	This section included 11 query types:
	Essays, Reports, reading and/or writing, referencing (including summarising for paraphrasing) writing Literature Reviews, writing up research, letter writing, writing up evidence for portfolios, case studies, dissertations, CVs.
Group 2 IT	This section included 10 categories of queries:
	Word, Excel, Access, Power-point, Windows, Email, Blackboard, Internet, Programming, Non-specific practical IT operational queries. SPSS.
Group 3 Research	This section had 1 query type:
	Gathering Information.
Group 4 Study Skills	This section included 4 query types:
	Study Skills, Time management, Presentations, Exams,
Group 5 General queries	This section included:
	Information given on other aspects of the university and/or redirected queries in the learning resource centre.

Qualitative Findings

The questionnaires were circulated in two phases. Phase 1 was from 1998–2000 and concentrated on the development of the SSC to try to identify students' needs and thus plan the practical development of the Student Skills Centre. The focus of Phase 2, which was from 2000–2002 was to try to extrapolate students' personal views of their progress in study skills (see Barkas 2008 for copies of questionnaires).

Findings from Phase 1- 1998–2000

These questionnaires focused on establishing what the students wanted from the SSC. To try to maximize possible return rates, different sampling and distribution methods were tried, as follows:-

1998–1999: 447 self-completion questionnaires were sent to those students who had visited the Student Skills Centre (SSC) on at least one occasion. The questionnaires were sent to students via their Schools, enclosing a self addressed return envelope. 39 responses were received.

1999–2000: 80 self-completion questionnaires were personally handed to a random sample of students who had attended the SSC on at least one occasion. 26 responses were received.

The responses from the questionnaires distributed over the two years were combined: 1998–1999 (39 responses) and 1999–2000 (26 responses). The combinations of 65 responses to the questionnaires were then evaluated for the formal research process. The extracts from the report are offered here as an overview of some of the key points. 27 of the 65 students attended the SSC more than twice and 13 attended more than three times. This pattern has continued, whereby if a student attended the Centre in the first year, they would call back for help in other years of their study. As discussed, helping students develop their writing skills was the dominant query in the recorded data. In terms of whether or not the students valued the help given 44/65 thought it helpful, 17 'very helpful' with one student marking it of 'no help at all' but returned over three times.

In response to the question: please list any additional services you would like the SSC to offer, examples of the categories of responses given were:

Sessions on coping with stress; Students past experiences of marks for reports etc. from the different schools, i.e. how would they improve it etc. including tutor feedback; SSC could offer more IT help; Longer opening hours.

The students' requests that were practical to respond to were IT support and longer opening hours. The Centre did not have access to individual courses' past papers.

In response to the questions: 'I would welcome any further comments you may wish to make about the SSC'.

The students who chose to complete this section did not write any negative comments, they viewed the support offered as positive. Three examples of typical comments were:

Booklets extremely helpful – even to my father studying on an MSc;.

I think it's a great offer and a lot more students should use it.

You do a great job!; SSC is a truly excellent service and I would have been lost without it. I have been given excellent support and advice each time I have visited.

Findings from Phase II Distribution of Questionnaires on Students' Study Skills

480 questionnaires were distributed over the two years 2000 to 2002. These surveys were also combined:-

Responses (n)		response rate (%)
2000–2001	033/200	16.5%
2001–2002	017/280	06.0%
Total	050/480	22.5%

A 5 point Likert scale was chosen for each of the sections on the questionnaire(ref) 1. weak; 2. fair; 3. good; 4. very good; 5. excellent.

I note some examples of the comments given in the four sections: reading, writing, English Language and writing essays and reports:

Reading

The categories for reading on the questionnaires were marked as: 2 weak; 12 fair; 17 good; 16 very good; 3 excellent.

One of the two students, who wrote that their reading skills were weak, also added a comment. He was on an Engineering Course and wrote that he did not read much:

Not very much

Typical responses from students who thought there reading skills were 'good' or 'very good' were:-

I have developed my reading skills with the help of handouts to direct me to articles which are useful. Also through the advice of my tutors;

Learnt how to use a book to gain its full advantage without reading the whole thing;

Since joining the university I've been reading a lot more for my research which has helped, but I still struggle a bit;

Having to read for modules, never read so much before, that is the way of development. I have got better – I think.

Findings from existing research into the links between reading and language skills was the foundation of the literacy task force initiatives taking place at the time (Standish, 2002) so it is interesting to see the similarity in the scale of responses. Obviously, it is not possible to offer any further comment without detailed content and context analysis of any reading material that was accessed.

Writing

The categories for writing on the questionnaires were completed as: 6 weak; 17 fair; 18 good; 7 very good; 2 excellent.

Two of the three students, who thought their writing skills were weak, wrote:

I feel more confident, learned about referencing and connection words such as however moreover etc:

Not a lot

Some examples of comments from students who thought their writing skills were fair or good are as follows:

From reading books and from information skill packs from SSC:

I have improved on different ways of developing arguments to also include reflection;

Developed over 3 years through trial and error, also by using the SSC for grammatical errors (sic). They have identified what I have been doing wrong. I have now corrected my writing style.

The students who thought their writing skills were 'very good' or 'excellent' wrote comments such as:

Hadn't wrote (sic) an essay before I came here now regularly getting Bs/2:1s I have developed my writing style to a certain extent. I understand that there is still more help guidance needed; Again – as with reading skills – both the demands of my course and help obtained from the SSC on different writing techniques have developed my writing skills since joining the university.

English Language

The section on English Language was organised over the 6 categories as shown in Table 14 below, so the results were as follows:-

Table 14. English language

English language	1. Weak	2. Fair	3. Good	4. Vgood	5. Excellent
Constructing Sentences	6	20	15	4	4
Grammar	10	17	14	3	4
Spelling	5	16	13	15	3
Punctuation	4	19	9	14	4
Paragraphs	5	17	17	10	3
Putting your ideas in order	12	14	13	8	2

There was no overall pattern to the students' thoughts about their English Language skills. There was, however, some correlation between the comments in the categories 'weak' and 'putting your ideas in order'. For example, one Human Resource Management student wrote that they thought their ability to construct sentences was weak and so too, was putting their ideas in order, which would seem understandable. As research into basic literacy has shown, barriers to learning are intrinsically linked to students' perceived level of language competence (Gittins, 1993). One student stated that:

There was no real class development except the SSC- I have just had to cope with my level of English

Of course, the issues of concern (Gittins, 1993) may not be related to all aspects of grammatical construction, as suggested by another student from a part-time Nursing course who thought her writing skills were 'fair to good' but 'use of grammar and putting ideas in order' were weak. She wrote:

> My language skills are more academic. Some words have developed in the use of academic writing, e.g. pertinent to...

The Engineering student who wrote 'not a lot' for his general writing skills, ticked the weak column in all the boxes and wrote the same comment:

> Not a lot

Some examples of the comments from the students who thought their general English Language writing skills were 'fair' or 'good', are as follows:

> Through reading and writing more.

> My English Language skills have developed by reading through journals which are recommended in the reading list.

> This has helped me to become more articulate.

More confident students, with a stronger sense of 'identity' in language usage, (Ivanic, 1997) had more control over the writing process, thought their English Language skills were 'very good' or 'excellent' , and wrote comments such as:

> Constant reading/writing have given me the confidence to speak this language. I feel good to know that I am able to put ideas in order and tell when others are making grammatical and other mistakes; Through own research, course requirements/guidelines on English Language and studying in general have all helped to develop my English Language skills.

One of the main findings from research into basic skills developments (Baker, 1978; Hunt, 2004), and particularly the English as a second language speaker, is the importance of self-esteem in coping with the idioms of phrasal or prepositional verbs that are characteristic of the English Language. As research into students' learning approaches has helped to show, more confident students will readily accept the need to practise. Whilst they are also more able to acknowledge areas for improvement, they will not necessarily equate weaknesses with a belief that their skills are deficient (Biggs, 1987; Devlin, 2002, Longden, 2002; Marton and Saljo, 1976).

Essays and Reports

The section on 'Essays' in the questionnaires were completed as follows: 7 weak; 26 fair; 10 good; 6 very good; 1 excellent.

The section on 'Reports' in the questionnaires were completed as: 11 weak; 23 fair; 12 good; 4 very good; 0 excellent.

Some examples from the comments are:-

Trial and error – I've done some good ones and some terrible ones. I'm not consistent at doing it.

Although I got good marks on my essays/reports, I still find I have to do at least 3–4 drafts.

These have developed through good tuition and attention to detail; Slowly and I still struggle; Through SSC services, reading and becoming more experienced.

Some students thought their essay skills were good, but report writing only fair, was noted by the following example comment:

Read study skills guides and looked at specimen essays/reports

Other students thought the reverse, and examples of three comments are:-

Essay writing – using lecturer's advice plus SSC booklets. Limited report writing so far.

Had not written a report before but essays have developed into a more mature style; SSC and communications and learning skills module helped me.

With regard to writing essays – yet again a combination of the content and demands of my course and help obtained from SSC on essay writing have developed my skills. Unfortunately, I am unable to comment on report writing skills as until now I have not been required to write reports – only essays. One of my modules this semester however does require the submission of a report. I have asked advice from SSC re. Report writing and the advice and information provided are excellent.

Interviews

From the questionnaires, students were asked if they would agree to a confidential Interview? 34 said 'Yes' and 16 said 'No'. The 34 students were all contacted by the notification they gave, telephone and/or electronic mail. A second request was made one month after the initial contact, 12 students were interviewed and their responses are discussed below.

Although a low number of students, the ratio of the responses does reflect the general take up of the SSC services over the University. The School of Health is the largest School, and user of the SSC, the School of Computing the smallest and less frequent use of the SSC is made by its students. The balance of the profile of students attending the SSC seemed to be more towards mature females.

Findings from the Interviews with Students

The total number of responses from the questionnaires to agree for an interview was 34. From this initial response, 23 agreed and were offered a confidential interview, with 12 students turning up at the appointed time. The other 11 did not turn up after a second request. The interviews were semi-structured, recorded and transcribed. The questions were pre-arranged in themes and divided into the 8 sections as shown in Table 15 (see Barkas, 2008 for a copy of the interview questions).

Table No. 15. Categorical sections of the interview questions

Section no.	Description of the section
1	The profile details: Gender, Age, Course of Study and School
2	General aspects of studying at the University
3	Course
4	Study Skills Development
5	Yearly Progress
6	Using the Student Skills Centre
7	Future Courses/Career
8	Any advice to potential students?

The questions in each section of the interview followed the same format. For example:

1a) What have you enjoyed the most about your course?
1b) Least?

Although too small a sample to offer generalised interpretations, the interviews did show the importance of writing skills development and offer an opportunity for further insight into the students' views of their own progress in study skills development. The profile details of the students who were interviews was 7 females, 5 males, and 3 were under 21 years of age and from the first and second year of study, the others were all 3rd years students.

The 12 Students were from the following schools and various programmes as noted: 1 Physiotherapy; 1 Diploma in Social Work; 1 Health Promotion; 1 Psychology; 1 Sociology; 1 HND IT & Business; 1 Masters in Multi-Media; 1 Graphic Design; 1 History; 2 Two Human Resource Management.

From section 2, 'general aspects of studying at the University' some of the responses were:

Interview question 1. Which university was your first choice?

The researched university was the first choice for nine students, second choice for two and third choice for 1 student.

Interview question 2. a) What have you enjoyed the most about studying at the University?

Students claimed they enjoyed their course, expressing it in personal terms such as: The digital imagery we are doing. It's very interesting and particularly related to my subject, photograph; More time to work on computers; The best part has been the learning experience, being away from home, meeting people and having the opportunity of a lifetime to do something I have always wanted to do. Making a new life for myself.

Section 3-Course

Interview question 1a) What have you enjoyed the most about your own choice of course?

Two examples of comments are:

Nothing wrong with the course. The time-table was well set up; Best? The variety of the course and the practical placements that we've been on, four in the second year and four in the third year.

b) least?

One student simply said:

Nothing.

Two students answered this by saying something positive about the course as in:

To be honest I can't think of anything that I have enjoyed the least about it. I have really enjoyed all of it; No...I wouldn't say there was. I have enjoyed every minute of it. Barring the odd tutor, everybody has been overly nice, you know, overly helpful...

One student did not like database tutorials (computer based tutorials -meaning self-directed learning on the computer with a printed guide)

Anything to do with tutorials. I don't find that a good way of learning. The tutorials are only as good as the person or people who have written them. They sometimes offload. I think this sort of learning programme is difficult to write because sometimes when you write it, you already know about it and you tend to assume there is some knowledge there rather than assume no knowledge and start from scratch...All the way there are bits missing...I found it better to go on-line and download them from other parts of the internet. There is a person who can help, but when you have one person to 20 or 30 students, it is difficult for the staff to accommodate everybody. They do their best. I'm not criticising the staff, I just find that a way of learning and certainly a way of teaching that I can't come to terms with.

One student said the course was very good but did not like the exams:

Nothing really. The exams probably least actually because I don't like doing 100% exams, especially 'cos this term I think most of them are.

Two of the interviewees' responses to the negative aspects were related to problems with internal communication and/or module demands. For example:

Probably lack of organisation and communication in the department. Messages being given to individuals rather than a letter being sent out to everyone. An example of this would be last week when a letter should have gone out to everyone who was about to finish their placement...

Although praising the facilities:

I think the facilities are particularly good, especially the Learning Resource Centre. It's great that so many PCs etc. are available and the library facilities and the little conference facilities are all really good and it's helped a lot as we have been studying.

One student said:

> The worst thing is, from an IT point of view, some of the library systems seems to be particularly difficult to negotiate for the average everyday student. It's fine for an IT person, like myself, but if you are really restricted with your computing knowledge...when you think the majority of students are using the Microsoft suite, then sensibly you would think that they would put it in the same place. But I find that they don't.

One student liked the geographical location the least:

> Least? The town. I don't like living in student accommodation. It's just extremely low standard I find. It's extremely bad. I feel unsafe. I don't like crime. It's just a totally different environment from what I'm used to at home. I mean I'm used to walking through the city at four o'clock in the morning, no worry, but here I don't go out by myself after nine.

Two students mentioned lack of car parking facilities, and 1 student, where the University was not the first choice said:

> Knowing that NWU is not the best university. Looking at the list of universities, and NWU is about ** something, this is itself demoralising and sometimes you ask the question will you be able to get a job when you graduate?

Car parking facilities is an ongoing issue for NWU and it was, at the time of writing in 2009, investigating this common complaint. Standing in the league tables, is of course, a much more complex issue. Criticisms of the tables are based on acknowledging the spurious nature of league tables, but maintaining or raising the position on publicly presented data is at the core of problems related to widening participation and keeping the 'standard' of a degree.

In answer to Interview question 3.1.c) Would you like to say anything else about your course? (prompt if necessary please state areas where is could be changed/improved?) The students answered that they had come to the Student Skills Centre for help, but some examples of other responses were:

> The course could be changed by incorporating more practical aspects i.e. skills that would help you in your work outside of the academic classroom. It is more theoretically based at the moment. Communication skills could be one of them that help you in your job later on. Debating skills could also be one as this is an essential part of the course.

Many programme tutors would argue that they do provide practical aspects, as noted by some of the positive comments in the above section relating to work placements, so without investigating the course content of the particular programme it is difficult to see whether this student's personal view had any practical validity.

Section 4- Study Skills Development

Interview question 4.1. Thinking about your own study skills development, what was the easiest/hardest?

Nine students stated meeting deadlines was the easiest part of their work, two mentioned essay writing, and one student said group work was the easiest.

Some examples of comments are:

I think you get out of the habit of essays when you get out of education;

My essay writing, I am used to doing reports because I did a GNVQ before this and it was report format all the time. I'm not used to doing essay writing. Hardest thing is when you do not know what is expected of you.

Some modules on the course do not always explain at the beginning what is required, and you have to go back and ask them, is this right? If it had been the case that they had explained everything clearly in the beginning, you could go on and do your own research. This is particularly connected to research. My dissertation is fine.

It is mainly the modules; I am quite pleased that I have met all my deadlines and not had to ask for an extension. I would not say it has been easy because I haven't studied for quite a while before coming to university although I did go back and do my A-levels, which got me back into a little bit of studying again.

The second part of Section 4 on study skills development asked students this question:

Interview question 4.2. Thinking now about each aspect of your study skills, what stands out the most in learning to write: essays, reports, research methods, presentation skills, would you like to say anything else that comes to mind?

Essays were mentioned the most frequently as noted in the following comments by 6 students:

Easiest? Anything to do with computers. Hardest? Just writing.

Essays – Don't like essays. Don't like the un-structuredness (sic) of them. Haven't done too many – we've mainly done reports.

Getting everything together, planning the essay, the content-things to put in, looking at the assessment criteria for marking so that you are covering everything. How to write an essay – my language, the English grammar and things like that.

Essays –presenting and putting across and arguing your point of view, and presenting the evidence and being able successfully to do that. More or less the same for reports.

Easiest – I find the essay writing and meeting deadlines no problem. I've got a good English background and my work experience means that I respect deadlines.

Essays – Knowing your subject and then learning more about your subject by looking up the books that have been recommended, and reference materials and then getting them together, finding what's relevant and try to stay focussed on the questions.

Reports- the comments were either that students liked them or they did not have to write them on their current module. Two students said:

> Reports I find a lot easier because they are clearly structured and you can answer each topic as you go along; Reports – I've never done a report.

Some examples from other aspects, about the easiest and hardest part of their course were given by three students:

> Easiest? Probably the amount of work. I mean everybody warned me there was going to be so much but I don't find that its...well...it's increased this year but it's not as much as I expected. Hardest? Getting into the assignment writing and style of learning here because it's very difficult for me...

> Hardest? The hardest thing for me was the Maths and in the first and second semesters, I had to have help to understand the mathematics because I wasn't coping with the module where maths was required.

> Hardest – learning the referencing system. Really struggling sometimes to think that you've got the commas in the right place and you've put the italics in the right place and because you know you're going to loose (sic) points if you haven't done it right, that caused a headache.

Section 5-Yearly Progress

Interview question 5.1. Thinking about your progress in your studies: Looking back over your year(s) what would you say was the easiest/hardest part of each year?

and

Interview question 5.2. In terms of your progress what do you think has been: your greatest/worst achievement?

> One student gave brief answers as follows:

> Easiest – using computers

> Hardest – tackling ideas

> Greatest achievement – getting to 'uni' and trying to finish this course

> Worst – essays

Another said:

> Easiest – doing less modules

> Hardest – I was doing computing for a year and switching to psychology was a big transition for me.

> My computer skills are always improving...and just generally getting through the degree because a lot of people drop out. Sometimes I think I am not doing very well but then you think, well, I am in year 3 and I must be OK. You've survived!

Worst – failing an essay. You know if you fail and you realise its no good and you don't have good comments you can use. Why did this fail? I mean, I wouldn't have handed it in if I had thought it was going to fail. It's a large de-motivating experience and it makes you feel awful really. Then when you are handing it in you are having to do an excellent essay because you thought the last one was good. This must be excellent but I will only get 40%. It can bring your whole grades down and it can overall make you feel awful.

One student referred directly to the course:

Hardest? The very first module. It was the Reformation. I found it a struggle probably because the majority had done it at A-level and I hadn't studied it whatsoever. I didn't know anything about Henry VIII and who he was. I'd never heard of him, so I found that quite an eye-opener.

Greatest achievement – I now go on the Access course and help other students, completely (sic. I can answer any of the questions on study skills, university life, how you progress, and you progress a lot, you do. I mean, when I look back on my essays from Year 1 now, there's a heck of a difference…Reading a book – it wouldn't enter my head to start at the front of a book any more. I go straight for the index…

The same student demonstrated how they had coped using a strategic approach:

Worst – when I get a grade under 60, I feel it's all pointless. I do, I think, what's the point? Especially, when a tutor will say 'I can't put it into words what's wrong with it'. And you'll say to them, 'If you can't who can?' you know. They'll give you something like a 59 and you'll say 'what did I need to get that other one mark?' 'Well I can't put it into works' and you could scream. You get really frustrated so you tend to find out which tutors' your style fits as you go along in the three years and that's how most students do it.

Section 6- Using the Student Skills Centre

Two students referred to their writing skills, as these two examples show:

It has helped with my grammar. I feel a lot more confident now and I feel like I am relying on it so much but I still like to come in to make sure I am doing the right thing. I feel that my writing style has improved and now I've got the intelligence bit, it's just putting it down on paper is my worst nightmare. It just feels like I am becoming more confident with it. It just feels that good.

I only came to the SSC for one period of time when I was doing quite badly in essay writing. It was all of a sudden my grade had dropped and they (the tutors) had commented that my grammar wasn't good and my punctuation wasn't good, and my general style wasn't good. I came to you and we worked through a large essay, step by step, week by week, and it stood me in good stead for the rest of them…

Some students made general points such as:

> Well, it has been a marvellous back up, because I can come here and I am treated like an adult, an adult that I am, (sic) instead of like a child...

Section 7- Future Courses/Career

Some examples are, related to the course:

> Modules for next year – we have already signed up for those.

Or the students' feelings about the tutors had a strong influence as in:

> I know what I'd like to do. I want to do modules that are of interest to me and obviously pertain to my work but are interesting, hopefully the tutors who are going to be stimulating and encouraging, so I will certainly be looking at who is doing what and who the tutors are because from past experience, I know I would not like doing modules where certain tutors that were taking them weren't inspiring to put it kindly. So that makes a big difference which is important. I think, yes, you want interesting material, (sic) you're wanting to learn interesting things but the tutor makes a big difference as well.

Section 8- Any Advice to Potential Students?

Three students suggested making the most of the resources, as demonstrated in their comments:

> Try to study more to find out more about the background of your course. Try to study and don't go to parties too much.

> To make the most of the facilities here. To grab every opportunity that comes along and use the library and learn how to use it properly. Students need to know about the Student Skills Centre – I think it's quite scary that there is a service here and people don't know about it.

> Make full use of the resources, because I wasn't aware of them when I first started really.

Summary of the Qualitative Research Findings

The percentage number of responses from the questionnaires for the first two years of Phase 1 was 14.5% and 22.5% for the second phase. The responses did show how the students were concerned about different aspects of their writing skills.

The students who had agreed to an interview were all regular users of the Students' Skills Centre. The average number of visits being twice per month for most students but two of the interviewees had received long term help with their writing skills over the course of one semester. Their answers did raise some further insights into potential disciplinary differences but, equally, the sample was too small to offer any generalisations. The sample did, however, highlight the importance of writing skills development and showed how the tutors in the Centre had supported them. The overall observation of the interviewees was how they had all demonstrated self-motivation in recognising how and why they needed help and had actively sought it.

The ethical issues in the study showed how complex the relationship to SSCs and subject based teaching have become. Whereas most tutors and management could see the value in optional, additional student support, they were also unwilling to acknowledge that there was no one generic writing exercise and/or style that could be adapted for every student from all the different courses.

Section 2 of 4: Quantitative Findings

The 3420 students' queries recorded were then classified into categorical data and some examples from the data analysis are given in this section. The findings from the qualitative research showed that the students' requests for help with writing were increasing, so the categorical data was analysed using statistical methods. The contingency table was created from the same variables as examined in the qualitative research, so any relationship between and among the different groups has been examined for interactions. In log-linear analysis the effects of more than one independent variable on a dependent variable is measured through the main and interaction effects (Everitt, 1977). The main effect is a significant difference between two or more means; it measures the mean change in the changes of the scores of a single independent variable, averaged over all combinations of levels of the other variables. The interaction effects measure the significant difference between two or more means. This shows that if there is a variation, it is not the result of a simple combination of the other independent variables. The interactions here are given to show the importance of the differences in the variables. The detail presented by the use of the log-linear analysis gave a breakdown of the nature of the students' requests and the importance of any relationship was shown by the use of confidence intervals. The use of interactions is presented graphically in a plot diagram which makes the data easier to see in visual form. The graphs are simple frequency line charts. The vertical axis represents scores on the dependent variable and the horizontal axis shows different levels of one independent variable. Each line on the plot graph shows another independent variable. If the lines are parallel, there is no interaction effect, if the lines are a different shape or cross, then the interaction can be tested for statistical significance (Brown, 1976; Everitt, 1977).

The side headings separate the explanations of each different aspect of the interpretations of the model. This formal objective style of writing is chosen to avoid the possibility of altering the meaning of the application of the statistical model if the syntax was changed.

Analysis of Categorical Data from 1999 to 2002

A sample of 3420 students were classified into A: Query (Writing, IT, General Query), B: Academic Year (99/00, 00/01, 01/02), C: Status (Full Time, Part Time), D: Gender (Female, Male) and E: Over 21 (Younger, Older), then they were tabulated into a 5-way contingency (Table No. 16).

Table No. 16. 3420 students were classified into A: Query, B: Academic Year, C: Status, D: Gender and E: Over 21. The observed frequencies are noted, with the expected frequencies written in the bracket. The confidence intervals are given in Table 17 in Appendix 2

Q.	Acad. year	Status							
		Full time				Part time			
		Female		Male		Female		Male	
		<21	>21	<21	>21	<21	>21	<21	>21
Wtg.	1999/ 2000	98.5 (98.2)	338.5 (337.5)	72.5 (72.7)	212.5 (213.5)	5.5 (7.1)	6.5 (6.1)	5.5 (3.9)	2.5 (2.8)
	2000/ 2001	112.5 (112.8)	443.5 (448.8)	36.5 (34.7)	195.5 (191.7)	0.5 (2.1)	55.5 (48.3)	0.5 (0.5)	9.5 (15.2)
	2001/ 2002	70.5 (69.6)	443.5 (446.2)	48.5 (50.2)	233.5 (230.0)	2.5 (1.4)	53.5 (52.8)	0.5 (0.8)	18.5 (20.1)
IT	1999/ 2000	4.5 (3.4)	17.5 (19.4)	0.5 (2.1)	12.5 (10.2)	2.5 (1.7)	2.5 (2.5)	0.5 (0.8)	0.5 (1.0)
	2000/ 2001	2.5 (1.4)	11.5 (13.6)	0.5 (2.6)	38.5 (35.5)	0.5 (0.0)	2.5 (2.0)	0.5 (0.0)	2.5 (3.9)
	2001/ 2002	45.5 (45.8)	143.5 (140.3)	73.5 (74.0)	159.5 (161.9)	0.5 (1.9)	32.5 (34.0)	4.5 (2.3)	29.5 (28.9)
Gen Q.	1999/ 2000	22.5 (22.9)	47.5 (47.6)	21.5 (20.7)	36.5 (36.8)	5.5 (5.6)	3.5 (2.9)	3.5 (3.8)	1.5 (1.7)
	2000/ 2001	17.5 (17.4)	67.5 (67.6)	3.5 (4.2)	23.5 (22.8)	0.5 (0.3)	7.5 (7.7)	0.5 (0.1)	1.5 (1.9)
	2001/ 2002	12.5 (11.5)	46.5 (42.1)	8.5 (7.9)	14.5 (20.6)	0.5 (1.8)	33.5 (37.7)	0.5 (0.9)	19.5 (13.6)

As the number of possible models is over 1000 in a 5 way contingency table, the best model was selected by a stepwise selection procedure using a conditional likelihood ratio test.

According to Table No. 16 above, the observed and expected frequencies are very similar, the adequacy of the model selected is tested by a goodness of fit test, i.e. likelihood ratio test, and the p-value for this test is 0.3835 (i.e. $\chi^2_{29} = 30.62$), so the null hypothesis cannot be rejected, where the null, H_0, and an alternative hypothesis, H_1, are as below:

H_0 : the model fits the contingency table well

H_1: the model does not fit the contingency table well

According to the goodness of fit test, the model selected explains the observed frequencies very well, as the p-value is 0.3835. If the model fitted is correct and the total sample size is large, then the above statistic has approximately an χ^2 distribution with degrees of freedom given by: (No of cells)-(No of parameters fitted). The model selected is attached in Appendix 1).

All the main effects and interactions were measured for the formal research, (Barkas, 2008) but for the purpose of illustration here, I have noted only the main effect due to query and academic year, as I was able to prove the queries on writing were increasing.

The main effects are the first interpretations of the model selected.

First Interpretations of the Model Selected

Interpretation of the Main Effect Due to 'Query'

When the main effects and interactions are found, marginal and partial association tests proposed by Brown (1976) are applied. For a test statistic, a conditional likelihood ratio test is used (see Barkas 2008). For example,

Model 1 $\log F_{ijklm} = u + u_{A(i)} + u_{B(j)} + u_{AB(i,j)}$

Model 2 $\log F_{ijklm} = u + u_{A(i)} + u_{B(j)}$

Model 2 is equivalent to model 1 when all the parameters $u_{AB(i,j)}$ are 0.

The conditional likelihood ratio statistic is approximately distributed as χ^2 under suitable conditions, e.g. all the parameters $u_{AB(i,j)}$ are 0 in the above example and the total sample size is large.

To find differences in the levels of a main effect or an interaction, a 95% confidence interval of parameters was used and this is shown in Table 17 in Appendix 2) According to the conditional test for marginal and partial associations, a significantly larger proportion of students had a writing query than any of the other queries at a significance level of 5%. The proportion of students asking about IT and those students with a general query are almost the same, (see Figure 1 and Table 17 in Appendix 2). Figure 1 shows the number of different queries for three years.

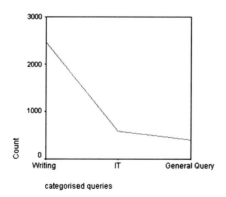

Figure 1. Collapsed line chart for 'Query'.

Interpretation of the Main Effect Due to 'Academic Year'

The proportion of students who attended the SSC, for study skills help in the year 00/01 was significantly smaller than that in year 99/00 at a significance level of 5%, but that in year 01/02 it was significantly larger than that in year 99/00 at a significance level of 5%, (see Figure 2 and Table 17 in Appendix 2). When analysing contingency tables, the null hypothesis is a model and the alternative hypothesis is the model under the null hypothesis plus a suitable u-term. If the conditional test is significant at a significance level of 5%, then there is an effect corresponding to the u-term from the existence of the main effect due to academic year. The SSC became much more popular in year 01/02. It seems that the interpretation is contradictory in Figure 7, however, the interpretations should be referred to the confidence intervals for the main effect terms of the model selected (See Barkas, 2008). For instance 95% confidence interval for the main effect due to academic year 99/00, 00/01 and

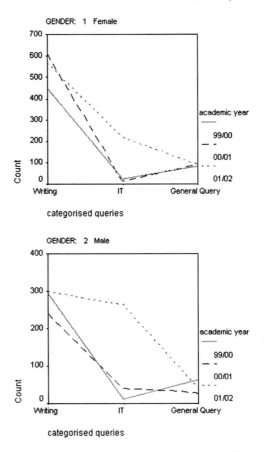

Figure 2. Collapsed multiple line chart for 'Query', 'Academic Year' and 'Gender'.

01 02 are (-0.288, 0/150), (-0.874, -0.370) and (0.475, 0.908), respectively (See Appendix 2, Tables 17, 18 and 19 inclusive). For the interpretation of main effects and interactions, a confidence interval for parameters, should be consulted, however, the number of estimated parameters are too many, especially for higher order interaction effects, so it is complicated. Therefore, it is easier to consult main and interaction plots for interpretation of the main and interaction effects and a plot graph was given for each of the parameters in the formal report (Barkas, 2008).

Interpretation of the Interaction Effect among 'Query', 'Academic Year' and 'Gender'

The interaction effect proves that with this data, male students use more IT than female students. Here, this tendency is slightly less than the first order interaction effect in the academic year 1999/2000. In the academic year 99/00, the ratio of male students to female students who attended the SSC with questions about IT was more than the first order interaction effect, i.e. the number of female students asking about IT in 99/00 was increased, (see Figure 2 and Tables 17, 18 and 19 in Appendix 2).

Summary of the Quantitative Findings

The findings from the qualitative research showed that requests for writing help were increasing, so the use of statistics was employed to evaluate the nature of this increase. The analysis of the contingency table confirmed this finding but also allowed the relationship of the different queries in terms of academic year, age, gender, status and query, to be explored in more detail and identified and clarified. For example, the results from the qualitative study showed that the increase in writing queries was mainly from mature, female students. This relationship however, was not confirmed by the statistical investigation. For female students, the ratio of younger to older students was almost the same as that for male students. In other words, there was no interaction between gender and over 21, so age and gender in terms of relationship to the type of query, was not related (Barkas, 2008) so although the qualitative research findings suggested there were more females over the age of 21 years asking for help with their writing, the statistical test showed that this was not the case.

The statistical inquiry also confirmed that the proportion of female students (including those under 21 years) with queries about writing was significantly greater than male students at a significant level of 5%. In the relationship of query to age, gender and status, however, it was possible to see in more detail from the use of the statistics where the difference in age against query was not always significant at a level of 5% (See Barkas, 2008).

The qualitative results showed that there were more full-time than part-time students attending the SSC, and this result was confirmed by the statistics. What was not clear from the qualitative research findings however, was the relationship of IT to writing queries and other queries. The statistical analysis showed that the ratio of male to female students for IT was larger than that for writing and general queries combined, but the ratio of males to females for writing and general queries was almost the same as the ratio of male to female students of all queries together.

The next section of the chapter explains how the interpretations of the evidence were then tested against a group of first year Law students.

Section 3 of 4: Summary of Findings from the Applied Study of First Year Law Students

The study was completed in three stages during the academic year 2003 to 2004.

Stage One examined the possible influences behind students deciding to stay or leave a course and to establish if there was any link to the level of students' writing skills. As the findings from the generic data (See Barkas, 2008) had shown the rise in students' requests for help with the development of their writing skills, the first level of the review of writing skills of the Law students was again analysed against the same criteria. Level 2 writing skills (GCSE A-C grades) using the Pathways model as noted in the previous chapter (See Barkas, 2008). A questionnaire was designed to check three aspects of possible influence behind the students' profile (See Barkas 2008 for copies of the questionnaire). The results were then analysed using an SPSS data base (SPSS 2005).

In Stage Two, students were invited to complete an electronic Writing Skills Check. The level of writing skills on the Electronic Writing Skills Self-Check are above GCSE at 'Starter' level, which is at a level 3 (GCE A Level/Key Skills Level 3) in the National Qualifications Framework. 91 students completed the electronic skills self-check between 11.30 and 13.00 hours on Tuesday 23 September, 2003 in Room A1.065 of NWU. 12 forms were spoiled, (sheets missing and/or no name) so the data from 79 completed forms were matched to the questionnaires and this information was entered into the data base. The print-outs were re-checked manually as some of the students had either omitted their names or printed out the incorrect page. In Stage Three, I obtained some examples of students' written work to assess against the Pathways model (See Barkas, 2008). The level of writing skills was then assessed and compared to the findings from the data base analyses. It was then possible to produce a Student Profile after the analysis of the written work was compared against the statistical data (see Barkas, 2008).

Section 4 of 4: Summary of Research Findings

The data served a number of purposes, it helped identify students who would benefit from additional writing support; it provided the First Year Law Course Tutors with a breakdown of the students' writing skills; the data analysis showed that the students' perceived views of their writing skills was higher than the level illustrated in the electronic self-check and written material presented.

The research question number 2 was: What is the literacy level/standard expected in HE?' The level expected in year 1 is Level 3 (GCE Advanced Level or equivalent, see Chapters 1 and 2) progressing to Level 4 in years 2 and 3. The generic results showed that the majority of students asking for help with their writing at the SSC, were writing at Level 2 or lower. The generic research questions 3, 4 and 5 were then applied to examine this issue further:

3) Do students understand the level/standard of writing in HE?
4) Do levels of literacy and notions of standards differ across the disciplines?
5) Can students be supported to achieve the level of literacy required?

In answer to these questions, the qualitative results in the generic study showed that students underestimate the demands of writing at HE. They also, generally, perceived their proficiency of writing to be of a higher standard than it actually was; each subject tutor has a different level and notion of the standard of writing required in their discipline but students can be supported to achieve the level of literacy required. The applied case study on a group of First Year Law students was then conducted to explore further the nature of these issues.

The first stage of the analysis examined the relationships between the variables recorded, which were: personal details, choice of course, reading and writing, use of English Language and level or proficiency in a sample of personal writing. The aim of the second stage was then to explore any relationship between the variables: students' personal profile; their entry qualifications; level of proficiency in writing; exam results and choice to leave the course. The findings from the research showed that the students' view of their writing skills was generally good or very good with 14 of the sample of 79 acknowledging their writing skills were weak or fair.

To identify the connection to the different aspects of the writing process, the groups were then combined into a three-way contingency table which was used to test the significance of the relationship between the groups. The results showed that there was a tendency for students who were concerned about the stages of their writing, to be concerned about their writing in general.

The students' personal view of their writing was then assessed against the writing criteria. When their writing was assessed against the criteria (GCSE Grade A-C/Key Skills Level 2/National Framework-Adult Literacy Proficiency Level 2 DfES/QCA 2002) their actual level was lower, with some students being a grade below their own expectation. The qualitative interpretations obtained through the assessment of the students' writing against the grade descriptors, was then checked by the use of statistical tests. The results supported the interpretative qualitative findings.

None of the students' level of writing in the questionnaire demonstrated a pass at GCSE Grade C+, with a further 15 students being assessed as below GCSE Grade C and 14 students were assessed as being borderline GCSE Grade C. That is, 63% (50 students) of the 79 students were assessed as either below or borderline the GCSE/Level 2 criteria. This level of proficiency in writing was, therefore, considerably lower than the NWU's minimum standard expected of Level 3 (GCE Advanced level or equivalent). The statistical significance of these results was then discussed against the outcomes of individual online skills checks, (see Barkas, 2008) then the findings were tested using the Wilcoxon Signed Ranked test. These results were then discussed in each table (see Barkas, 2008). A sample of written work pre-pared by 29 students was then further examined to identify the level of proficiency in writing skills (See Barkas, 2008).

The results of the data were then analysed against the final year exam results with destinations cross-tabulated to each student (See Barkas, 2008). Of the sample of 79 students, 14 students who expressed concern about their writing were recorded as re-sitting several modules, 9 were noted as re-sitting the first year, 11 students withdrew from the course and 45 continued into the second year. The conclusions of this case study, therefore, support the findings from the generic research which showed that on entry, many students were not demonstrating writing skills at the required entry level of Level 3 (GCE Advanced Level). As stated in the qualitative analysis, the results from the study on the First Year Law students, also confirmed, however, that students with a minimum entry standard of Level 2 (GCSE or its equivalent) can be supported to improve their competence in writing. Students with an entry proficiency level of 2 or below were also able to improve their level of proficiency. The end of year results, however, showed that of the 11 students who chose to leave the course, 7 of them were assessed at Level 1. At the end of the formal research study, quantitative data was maintained and the number of students visits to the SSC continued to show an annual increase.

Between the Text Comment

During the period shortly after the formal research was completed, attention was given to a UCU challenge over the HERA team's role appraisal's failure to accept the complexity of the students' requests for help in the SSC. This was an ongoing process in 2010, but the issues discovered in the research remained unacknowledged by most of the academic staff and management in the NWU. It seemed both the managers and many of the academic staff shared a lack of interest in the problems the SSC presented. This could be for a number of reasons. It may be because they did not see the SSC as important to them, or because they believed that 'their' students did not attend the Centre. Further research is required to find out why, but who would have the interest to do it? The academic tutors in the SSC worked for 3 of their weekly total of 18 teaching hours, and during the decade of the research, the nature of the team changed on a regular basis, so lack of continuity prevented the possible collaboration on research projects. This may change if the management of the SSC was moved back into an academic team. Lecturers were also not interested in other subjects, giving support to Becher and Trowler's (2001) view of the differ-ences between academic tribes. I am an optimist by nature, but I must admit the continued negative attitudes towards myself and my colleagues was demoralising. Over the years of the research, I repeatedly made attempts to bring the management of the SSC under the remit of the Education Section (the original home) that became part of the School of Social Sciences and Law. I felt like the donkey character in the film 'Shrek' (Shrek, 2001) that jumps up and down all the time. (If you haven't seen it, this comment does not mean anything to you, but it is comical and worth seeing whether or not you watch it with children). At least that way, we would be surrounded by other academics who would, I hope, understand at least some of the issues students presented at the SSC and together, we could set about more effective solutions to students' learning needs. Perhaps this too, would prove to be wishful thinking. I am referring to the donkey in Shrek (2001) but hopefully, I do not always look quite so startled.

End of Comment

The next chapter provides the concluding arguments to the issues explored in the book.

CHAPTER 7

CONCLUSION

The collective manifestations of the insanity that lies at the heart of the human condition constitute the greater part of human history. It is to a large extent the history of madness. If the history of humanity were the clinical case history of a single human being, the diagnosis would be: chronic paranoid delusions, a propensity to commit murder and acts of extreme violence and cruelty against his perceived "enemies"–his own consciousness projected outward; criminally insane, with a few brief lucid intervals (Tolle 2005, 11–12).

Conformity may give you a quiet life; it may even bring you a University Chair. But all change in history, all advances, comes from nonconformists. If there had been no trouble makers, no Dissenters, we should still be living in caves (Taylor, 1993, 14).

Introduction

I start this final chapter with two quotes. The first from Tolle (2005) has been chosen as despite the 'wealth of nations' (Brown et al., 2008; Sandel 2009) it depicts the brutal conflicting tensions at the core of society today. The second quote by A. P. J. Taylor illustrates that any change that has occurred in society has been because people have disagreed and refused to conform, so change has not always been transitory or without conflict. The research into the SSC does not align with the dominant view of what the work of the centre should be, so the senior managers and academic staff see my attempts to draw attention to the problems as simply a nuisance, and I am castigated as the "dissenter", just another trouble maker, (Taylor 1993, 14). The reluctance of many universities to stand against the dominance of the ruthlessness of the market, (within the topic of role of higher education), depicts a manifestation of the "the history of madness" (Tolle, 2005). The old traditional universities have been attacked for not changing enough because throughout the decades they have remained solid and true to their belief in the power of the content of knowledge. Ironically, it is this very appreciation of knowledge that will bring about the much needed change in the current approaches to higher education (Bligh, 1990; Green, 1997; Young and Muller, 2010).

Although universities have been successful in their widening participation strategies, many of them have not given sufficient attention to the multiple aspects of the differentiated learning needs of an increasing student populace. The managers of some universities, however, would claim that they have introduced numerous strategies to help students succeed on their courses. These initiatives range from embedding learning skills in programmes of study, providing extra support during the first year of study to offering centralised support centres (Thomas et al., 2003; Wingate, 2007). In this book, I have drawn on the research conducted into a centralised students' skills centre (SSC) to argue that although SSCs were well intentioned, they were poorly conceptualised and fail to address the educational needs of students. Before SSCs were introduced into universities their conceptual framework, responsibilities and boundaries would have been seen as impossible if, at the beginning, the right questions had been asked, such as: 'what can SSCs offer help in?'; 'how can SSCs limit what they do?'; 'what qualifications and experience will the staff need?' and most importantly of all, 'how can the SSC help?' A decade after the introduction of the SSC at NUW, these questions remained unanswered and the model of the SSC still existed (Barkas, 2008).

In post-1992 universities, SSCs sprang up like little mushrooms throughout the country as a 'knee-jerk' response to the 1997 Dearing Report's requirement for graduates to have 'key-skills' for employability. The contested issues surrounding the nature and content of these 'key-skills' dominated the literature in the late 1990s and the early part of the 2000s, whereby the emphasis in the discourse then shifted from key to employment skills (Ainley, 2000; Hager Hodkinson, 2009, Hyland, 2003; Preece and Godfgrey, 2009; Young and Muller, 2010). The findings of research into these *skills* showed that although they are important, they are subject and situation specific, and the ability to recognise if, how and when transferability would be applicable, is in fact a personal competence and not a general skill (Ainley 2000; Hyland, 2003). The findings from the extensive research however, did nothing to diminish the appeal of generic skills that despite any proven validity have gained widespread appeal over the past two decades (Bernstein, 2000). This was because of the desire for a codification of knowledge (Ainley, 2000; Young, 2009) made possible through the enforcement of managerialism in higher education (Kenny, 2009; Winter, 2009).

This final chapter will now be separated into two sections. The first section provides an outline of the issues that have been discussed in the book. The second section then offers a summary of the arguments presented in the previous chapters.

Section 1

Over the past few decades, the belief that an increased number of graduates in the workforce will automatically mean economic competitiveness of a society has eclipsed the intrinsic value of knowledge and a higher education. Despite the success of widening participation strategies employed by universities, the new utopia of a highly skilled, graduate workforce has not yet arrived. Instead, in the early 2000s, the world was entrenched in a recession (Duncan, 2008).

These global concerns affect the character of universities as they juggle with their own identity and their position in the league tables of other universities. It is possible to argue they have been forced into the business model by the market. It is however, equally possible to claim that they have helped create the market by their choice of a market-based structural model (Ainley, 2000; Argyris and Schon, 1996;

Barnett, 1990; Brown et al., 2008; Parry, 2005). Whatever argument is favoured, however, the tensions of survival, cooperation and competition coexist. In the past two decades, universities' identities have changed and some groups of universities have formed alliances. In 1994 a group of 19 universities formed an alliance and some other higher education institutions (HEIs) have formed links through their similar missions (Universities UK, 2010). The term 'elite' in the United Kingdom relates to the 20 traditional pre-1992 and research intensive universities, termed the Russell Group. Despite the economic recessions and political manipulations, these old, traditional universities have survived the snipes and snares of popular trends. The debates about elitism in the specialised literature may be strong and long-lasting, but no matter how the process is challenged and the traditional universities are encouraged to open up their admission system, the practical realities remain. There are only so many students who can be accommodated in any one institution and in a 'free-market' the wealthier and/or more successful institutions can choose whom they want to accept and thus defend their decisions in any way they see fit. In this book, I have not attempted to question their views. Students Skills Centres do not exist in these establishments, so my research would probably be of no interest to anyone working or studying in them.

I revisit my analytical metaphors one last time in this concluding chapter; SSCs are worlds away from the *universes* of the elite universities; in turn, the traditional universities as *institutions* are also in a different galaxy from the post-1992 institutions. This is not to suggest that the value is always higher in the traditional universities, but it has to be accepted, that it is different. In the twenty-first century, the global business opportunities have been accompanied with global terrorism and wars over ideas (Tolle, 2005). Sandel (2009, 2) has suggested that the "era of the market dominance", in what he terms "market mimicking governance" has come to an end because the current financial crises "has discredited market triumphalism in both its laissez-faire and Neoliberal versions." Sandel (2009, 2) argues that there must be radical change in societies to bring about a revival of moral and civic virtue within a political system that recognises them. The new politics, he asks:-

> What might such a politics look like? Unlike market-driven politics, a politics of the common good invites us to think of ourselves less as consumers, and more as citizens. Here's why this matters. Market-mimicking governance takes people's preferences as given and fixed. But when we deliberate as citizens, when we engage in democratic argument, the whole point of the activity is critically to reflect on our preferences, to question them, to challenge them, to enlarge them, to improve them. Every successful movement of social or political reform has done more than change the law. It has also changed attitudes and dispositions, what Tocqueville called the "habits of the heart."

The renewal of moral and civic virtues in a politics of the common good (Sandel 2009) would hopefully, therefore, provide the necessary move away from the market dominance and release the pressure on universities to respond. This would then provide the supportive background for universities to restructure and rebuild to enable them to focus on returning to "knowledge institutions" (Coffield 2000; Duke 2002; Young 2009) thus providing a higher education system that yes, does address the need for a successful economy but also provides for a moral and civic good (Sandel, 2009, 3). The current collapse of the global market and the tensions in society do much to suggest that the over-emphasis on commodities has not been the right approach. Over the past ten years, the researched institution has been engrossed in its own battle for ideas, with the purpose of higher education as a business, crushing everything else in its wake. The fall-out from this distortion in the discourse has been a complex and contradictory structure of management and systems. On the one hand everything about higher education is measured through subject and discipline specific domains (Rowland, 2003) but on the other, these strict subject boundaries miraculously disappear when the managers want to talk of generic writing and study skills (Barkas, 2008).

These dilemmas are at the core of universities reluctance to face up to the problems presented by widening participation, regardless of how desirable opening up access to higher actually is. At different periods over the past twenty years research into remedial approaches has demonstrated how inappropriate it has been to claim that study skills are "divorced from subject content and knowledge" (Wingate, 2006, 459). Nevertheless, the belief that "bolt-on" (Bennett et al., 2000) non-subject specific, writing and study skills courses are the answer to students' learning needs, unfortunately reiterates again, the normalisation of diversification during cultural change (Bernstein, 2000) in the belief that knowledge is a manageable, codifiable, external, objective body of facts (Gamache, 2002; Young 2009; Young and Muller, 2010).

I have argued that the issues uncovered in the day-to-day work of the SSC reflect at the ground level of *student support* the larger challenges faced by universities. I focussed my study on one SSC in a post-1992 university to show how issues in helping students with their writing and study skills, despite the convincing rhetoric, unearthed deep seated prejudice to the notion of skills development and cross-institutional teaching. It is as if the research conducted over the past fifty years, into the complexity of skills and academic literacy has never taken place (Gee 1996, 2000; Hyland, 2004; Monroe, 2002; Wilson, 2009). It has been argued in this book that one of the unintended consequences of successful widening participation strategies has been increased pressure on universities to provide writing support at all levels of study. Students, however, can be supported to improve their proficiency in standards of writing, but SSCs are not the answer, they never were and never will be because the arguments for their existence are based on illusions.

Section 2

In this book, I reflected on research into students' requests for help at a Students' Skills Centre (SSC) to explore how and why differentiated values of the role of learning and teaching in higher education have developed. I have claimed that the work of SSCs encapsulates in a very small way, the extensive paradoxes and ironies that have developed during widening participation policies in higher education. From the longitudinal study of the SSC, it has been possible to examine some brief 'snapshots in time' to illustrate how widely held views, without proven validity, have gained extensive cultural acceptance. This normalisation process allows the beliefs to develop with little, if any, questioning of their applicability in a given context (Bernstein, 2000). The irony is the different viewpoints seem to be perpetuated in a 'world' of their own, within what I have metaphorically described as 'multiple-parallel universes' (Chown, 2007). I have argued that behind each of these different views, are complex and contested theories, and at any given point, the perpetuators of the various beliefs are like aliens in a new world, they are simply not "reading each other" (McCormack 1994; Neuman, 2001) as they wrongly presume that their words mean what they claim (Lum, 2004). The resulting confusion can be depicted by examining the nature of students' requests for help with their studies at an SSC. The managers of New World University (NWU) are so caught up in their responses within the language of the discourse of its management of the business of higher education, that they denied or refused, to acknowledge the possibility that there just might be more to the work of SSCs than they originally envisaged. The research conducted at NWU would therefore, support the work of Winter (2009) when he examined the schisms that result in managerialistic approaches to learning. The study of the students' requests for help at the SSC, also contributes to the knowledge of how the complexity of 'writing in, and across, the disciplines', despite many decades of research (Haggis 2009) is still not widely accepted in the field of research into learning and teaching in higher education (Baynham, 2000; Hyland, 2004; Lea and Stierer, 2000; Monroe, 2002).

The senior managers' priorities in NWU are related to managing the university as a business organisation. They do this according to their interpretation of their status and role responsibilities (Henkel, 2000). This means that their interpretation of what is meant by 'skills' could be widely different to the actual requests for help expressed by the students in the SSC. Equally, the 'skills and knowledge' necessary for the SSC tutor to address the students' learning needs is dismissed as being of a *low-level* nature. If the subject course leaders are responding to the needs and skills of 'their students', what is envisaged as generic and/or operational help in SSCs, is sometimes encapsulated as the responsibility of the manager of whichever building the SSC is located. Some universities locate the SSC in student services, social sciences or libraries (Thomas et al., 2003). A key difference between institutions lies in which management structure the SSC falls. In most institutions, regardless of the physical location of the SSC, the study and/or writing support is organised and managed from within an academic team that is usually within an education, social science or linguistics group (Crème and Lea, 1997; Ganobcsik-Williams, 2006, Haggis 2006; Lillis, 2006; Neuman, 2001; Wingate, 2007). The difficulty at NWU was that the SSC was moved from an education team to the management structure of the library, thus physically embracing the senior management's view that work in the SSC was generic within a systemic operational facility (Tait, 2000). From this single decision, every other aspect of the complexity and difference of students learning needs within any subject magnified exponentially (Barkas, 2008). As an ever increasing number of students attended the SSC, the management of NWU claimed it was a success, but the truth of the situation was that the increasing number of students provided evidence to argue that the systems in place in their subject were either insufficient or unsuitable. Ironically, an institutional audit of NWU took place in during the final stages of the research and the auditors of the report noted that "in-depth academic skills" were provided in the SSC, but not a single member of the audit team spoke to the staff in the SSC, so we did not know how they came to this conclusion. This statement may suggest there is documentary evidence somewhere in the organisation that they referred to that acknowledged that "in-depth academic skills" are provided in the SSC. If this was true, why did the management of NWU not accept the complexity of the SSC and continue to deny the true nature of the diversity and 'depth' of the subject specific nature of students' queries and why did they continue to discredit the evidence in their own institution? There was, after all, 12 years of it. Perhaps it was not intentional; perhaps the managers saw the other aspects of their workload as being of a more important nature.

So once again, the *issues* presented by the SSC were a low priority on their list of objectives. The managers are able to reconcile their lack of engagement in the problems presented by the SSC because they too remain convinced that their *world view* is the one that matters most. In the busy day-to-day *business* of running the university, the subject course leaders are responsible for ensuring their programme of study is conducted within their stated course outcomes and meets the institution's learning and teaching standards. Their focus is on their subject and they see no reason to concern themselves with other subject dilemmas (Becher and Trowler, 2001). So the result of this situation was that nobody wanted to accept responsibility for the issues the SSC presented, with each sector of the organisation, be it the senior managers or the academic staff. They all claimed "it was not their problem" (Brink 2009, 27) yet ironically, they still wanted to retain a facility to direct students too, for whatever reason but they did not want to spend their time to meet with the SSC staff to find out, if and how the centre could help. The hypocrisy of this attitude can be illustrated by the fact that some academic staff would send students to the SSC for help to write their 4000 word essays or 10,000 word dissertations. The subject tutor claimed they would be willing to look at a draft of 200 words of the essay but the student had to find out how to write the other 3800. Or in terms of the dissertation, they only had time to read through one chapter. The issues over the dissertations were exceedingly complex, and simply start from the basic question "what is the role of the SSC in relation to the dissertation supervisor?" In these situations, the students sought the guidance of the staff in the SSC, who may not have been from the subject area of the student's course. The time, content and reality of helping these students was recorded in detail, depicting how subjects embrace quite different linguistic concepts of what constitutes evidence and argument (Lea and Stierer, 2000; Young and Muller, 2010).

In the academic year 2007–2008 1222 students made 2096 visits to the centre. On average, the current staffing model can cope with an annual cohort of about 1000 students, but the number of repeat visits has also risen. In terms of repeat visits over the decade, there has been a steady annual increase of between 8 and 19%. The increasing numbers of students using the centre was interpreted by the management of NWU as a success. In their view, demonstrating another of their efficient operating systems, (Kenny, 2009) but in reality the numbers displayed the opposite. The number of students wanted help at the SSC that should have been provided by the subject tutors on their specific course. During the research period, I tried repeatedly to engage various parties in the researched institution to investigate the practicality of its minimum or threshold standards and also search for different methods of supporting students through the curriculum 'on course'. In early 2010, I have not yet succeeded in encouraging any of the managers or the subject tutors to show an interest in the problems presented by the SSC.

Higher education institutions (HEIs) have a number of options available to them to help them embrace the challenges the needs of a diverse student populace present, but ignoring the complexity of SSCs, should not be one of them. The senior managers, some academic staff and the personnel section must embrace the fact that their commodification (Ainley, 1994) of the role of the SSC is both deeply flawed and tragic. It stands in the way of any possible positive development of the curriculum that could provide a much more effective way of meeting the students' needs, as the evidence from the research into the SSC presents (Barkas, 2008). The loyalty academic staff have to their subject (Becher and Trowler, 2001) is intertwined with their attitude to knowledge and skills, and who, and how these should be taught, that equally has a differentiated relationship within and across the post-16 educational sector. Over the decade of the research the relationship between further and higher education sectors remained complex. Although widening participation presented many opportunities for the two sectors to work more closely together, these chances were not explored (Ainley 2000; Bathmaker and Thomas 2009; Parry 2009). An option now may be to revisit the possibilities open to both further and higher education. For example in the 1980s 'Access to Higher Education Courses' provided students with a course of study to prepare them for higher education (Parry, 1995). In their attempts to 'widen participation' universities have encroached on many aspects of further education's provision, resulting in disagreements about what is possible in either sector and whether or not, they should be separate, cooperative or combined institutions. It may be more productive to work together to find solutions rather than continue to focus on disagreements (Ainley, 2000; Bathmaker and Thomas 2009; Lucas 2004; Parry 2009; Parry, Davies and Williams 2004). Other options may involve one, or several changes to universities existing admittance criteria and/or course structure; such as introducing a stipulation that potential students must either demonstrate their proficiency in reading and writing to Level 3 (GCE Advanced Level, QAA, 1992) or undertake a mandatory, subject specific, writing module. Although 'skills modules' exist in many course programmes, most are currently of a generic nature and a clearer emphasis on how students should write about knowledge in a given subject would help students understand what is required. The students requiring remedial writing support could also be offered more help. Perhaps one of the first considerations must be the acceptance that any student's ability to develop 'academic literacy' in a given subject is the responsibility of the subject course tutor, and there is no generic writing style that will 'fit all subjects' (Gee, 2002).

Conclusion

In the meantime, SSCs may be viewed as micro-representative units that demonstrate all the issues resulting from successful strategies for widening participation in higher education. They reveal on a small scale the contradictions inherent in the current university system. The problems encountered by SSCs show how the research that disputed the transferability of key skills, particularly in relation to language, has largely been ignored and the work of SSC tutors in a cross-institutional, multi-disciplinary role is dismissed as second-rate support which is of insignificant value to modular teaching. The skills deficit thinking that is behind the mythical role of SSCs is then reflected in the emphasis on skills for employability that has continued against the backdrop of the research into knowledge-based economies that reveals how vulnerable societies are when they rely on the fickle nature of global trading (Brown et al., 2008; Sandel, 2009). Inherent in this approach is the problem that the continuation of SSCs prohibits further development of the curriculum to ensure claims to inclusion are real (Slee, 2001), so the most effective outcome would be to work towards a different model until practical, subject specific, alternatives are in place, thus rendering the SSC obsolete but in the meantime, SSCs very existence per-petuates the illusion of the applicability of genericism (Bernstein, 2000). An education for all should include all (Slee, 2001). As these new initiatives are instigated, the complexity of SSCs must be acknowledged and their function in providing a teaching role, accepted. The findings from the extensive research into writing in and across the disciplines must also be considered and built into the subject based, higher education curriculum. Equally, the influence of information communications techno-logy on the centrality of written and spoken language must be addressed, if students' proficiency in literacy is to be of a sufficient level to enable them to put into words the critical language awareness demanded of a *higher education*.

Students do have complex learning needs but acquiring knowledge at a higher level is difficult. It requires discipline and concentration of the mind. If I tried to qualify these assertions I would need to start writing another report about the nature of knowledge and perhaps define what we mean by *intelligence*. Intelligence on this or on another planet may be the topic of another book, but it will not be written by me. I just hope that I am not submitting a revision of this work as a second edition in a few years time because developments to replace SSCs had not been attempted. Unfortunately, after over 12 years, at the time of writing in early 2010, nothing had yet changed, but in the previous year, new managers had been employed at NWU so forever the optimist, I hoped to encourage one of them in the School of Social Sciences and Law to at least examine the findings of the research into the SSC, with a view to offering some support to help me bring about effective change. Perhaps the effects of the recession would also mean that some academic staff at NWU would have fewer students to work with, so they could spend more time in individual tutorials or they too, could help develop an inclusive curriculum; perhaps not.

Between the Text Comment

I hope the story ends happily in that SSCs finish on a high note and the issues they present are addressed from within the subjects under study. After all, universities do offer a *higher education* and we, as a society still value that, don't we?

End of comment. End of the Story of the SSC.

APPENDIX 1

THE FOLLOWING MODEL WAS SELECTED

$$\log F_{ijklm} = u + u_{A(i)} + u_{B(j)} + u_{C(k)} + u_{D(l)} + u_{E(m)} + u_{AB(i,j)} + u_{AC(i,k)} + u_{AD(i,l)} +$$

$$u_{AE(i,m)} + u_{BC(j,k)} + u_{BD(j,l)} + u_{BE(j,m)} + u_{CD(k,l)} + u_{CE(j,m)} + u_{DE(l,m)} +$$

$$u_{ABC(i,j,k)} + u_{ABD(i,j,l)} + u_{ABE(i,j,m)} + u_{BCE(j,k,m)} + u_{BDE(j,l,m)}$$

where F_{ijklm}, u, $u_{A(i)}$, $u_{B(j)}$, $u_{C(k)}$, $u_{D(l)}$, $u_{E(m)}$, $u_{AB(i,j)}$, $u_{AB(i,j)}$, $u_{AC(i,k)}$,

$u_{AD(i,l)}$, $u_{AE(i,m)}$, $u_{BC(j,k)}$, $u_{BD(j,l)}$, $u_{BE(j,m)}$, $u_{CD(k,l)}$, $u_{CE(j,m)}$, $u_{DE(l,m)}$,

$u_{ABC(i,j,k)}$, $u_{ABD(i,j,l)}$, $u_{ABE(i,j,m)}$, $u_{BCE(j,k,m)}$ and $u_{BDE(j,l,m)}$ are, respectively,

the expected frequency for (i,j,k,l,m) cell, overall mean effect, the main effect
of the i th category of variable A (i.e. Query), the main effect of the j th category
of variable B (i.e. Academic Year), the main effect of the k th category of
variable C (i.e. Status), the main effect of the l th category of variable D (i.e.
Gender), the main effect of the m th category of variable E (i.e. Over 21), the
first order interaction effect between the i th and j th categories of variables A
and B, the first order interaction effect between the i th and k th categories of
variables A and C, the first order interaction effect between the i th and l th
categories of variables A and D, the first order interaction effect between the i th
and m th categories of variables A and E, the first order interaction effect
between the j th and k th categories of variables B and C, the first order
interaction effect between the j th and l th categories of variables B and D, the
first order interaction effect between the j th and m th categories of variables B
and E, the first order interaction effect between the k th and l th categories of
variables C and D, the first order interaction effect between the k th and m th
categories of variables C and E, the first order interaction effect between the l th
and m th categories of variables D and E, the second order interaction effect
among the i th, j th and k th categories of variables A, B and C, the second
order interaction effect among the i th, j th and l th categories of variables A, B
and D, the second order interaction effect among the i th, j th and m th

categories of variables A, B and E, the second order interaction effect among the j th, k th and m th categories of variables B, C and E, the second order inter-action effect among the j th, l th and m th categories of variables B, D and E.

(Guidance on statistical model and related figures, Yanagisawa, 2002 cited in Barkas, 2008, 91).

APPENDIX 2

Table No. 17. Estimate and 95% confidence limits of the parameters
(overall effect and main effects)

u term	Estimate of u	Lower 95% confidence limit of u	Upper 95% confidence limit of u
u (Overall effect)	2.275	2.113	2.438
$u_{A(1)}$ (Writing)	1.023	0.815	1.231
$u_{A(2)}$ (IT)	-0.691	-0.944	-0.439
$u_{A(3)}$ (General Query)	-0.331	-0.558	-0.105
$u_{B(1)}$ (1999/2000)	-0.069	-0.288	0.150
$u_{B(2)}$ (2000/2001)	-0.622	-0.874	-0.370
$u_{B(3)}$ (2001/2002)	0.691	0.475	0.908
$u_{C(1)}$ (Full Time)	1.301	1.138	1.463
$u_{C(2)}$ (Part Time)	-1.301	-1.463	-1.138
$u_{D(1)}$ (Female)	0.261	0.098	0.423
$u_{D(2)}$ (Male)	-0.261	-0.423	-0.098
$u_{E(1)}$ (Younger)	-0.889	-1.051	-0.727
$u_{E(2)}$ (Older)	0.889	0.727	1.051

Table No.18. Estimate and 95% confidence limits of the parameters
(first order interaction effects)

u term	Estimate of u	Lower 95% confidence limit of u	Upper 95% confidence limit of u
$u_{AB(1,1)}$	0.051	-0.215	0.318
$u_{AB(1,2)}$	0.598	0.269	0.926
$u_{AB(1,3)}$	-0.649	-0.933	-0.365
$u_{AB(2,1)}$	-0.460	-0.825	-0.096
$u_{AB(2,2)}$	-0.578	-0.965	-0.191
$u_{AB(2,3)}$	1.038	0.722	1.354
$u_{AB(3,1)}$	0.409	0.121	0.697
$u_{AB(3,2)}$	-0.020	-0.370	0.331
$u_{AB(3,3)}$	-0.389	-0.707	-0.072
$u_{AC(1,1)}$	0.350	0.142	0.558
$u_{AC(1,2)}$	-0.350	-0.558	-0.142
$u_{AC(2,1)}$	-0.150	-0.403	0.102
$u_{AC(2,2)}$	0.150	-0.102	0.403
$u_{AC(3,1)}$	-0.200	-0.426	0.026
$u_{AC(3,2)}$	0.200	-0.026	0.426
$u_{AD(1,1)}$	0.130	-0.078	0.339
$u_{AD(1,2)}$	-0.130	-0.339	0.078
$u_{AD(2,1)}$	-0.275	-0.527	-0.022
$u_{AD(2,2)}$	0.275	0.022	0.527
$u_{AD(3,1)}$	0.144	-0.082	0.370
$u_{AD(3,2)}$	-0.144	-0.370	0.082
$u_{AE(1,1)}$	-0.022	-0.230	0.186
$u_{AE(1,2)}$	0.022	-0.186	0.230

Table No.18. (Continued)

$u_{AE(2,1)}$	-0.137	-0.390	0.115
$u_{AE(2,2)}$	0.137	-0.115	0.390
$u_{AE(3,1)}$	0.159	-0.067	0.385
$u_{AE(3,2)}$	-0.159	-0.385	0.067
$u_{BC(1,1)}$	-0.097	-0.316	0.122
$u_{BC(1,2)}$	0.097	-0.122	0.316
$u_{BC(2,1)}$	0.271	0.019	0.522
$u_{BC(2,2)}$	-0.271	-0.522	-0.019
$u_{BC(3,1)}$	-0.174	-0.390	0.043
$u_{BC(3,2)}$	0.174	-0.043	0.390
$u_{BD(1,1)}$	0.003	-0.216	0.221
$u_{BD(1,2)}$	-0.003	-0.221	0.216
$u_{BD(2,1)}$	0.061	-0.191	0.312
$u_{BD(2,2)}$	-0.061	-0.312	0.191
$u_{BD(3,1)}$	-0.063	-0.280	0.153
$u_{BD(3,2)}$	0.063	-0.153	0.280
$u_{BE(1,1)}$	0.657	0.439	0.876
$u_{BE(1,2)}$	-0.657	-0.876	-0.439
$u_{BE(2,1)}$	-0.477	-0.729	-0.225
$u_{BE(2,2)}$	0.447	0.225	0.729
$u_{BE(3,1)}$	-0.180	-0.397	0.036
$u_{BE(3,2)}$	0.180	-0.036	0.397
$u_{CD(1,1)}$	-0.076	-0.239	0.086
$u_{CD(1,2)}$	0.076	-0.086	0.239
$u_{CD(2,1)}$	0.076	-0.086	0.239
$u_{CD(2,2)}$	-0.076	-0.239	0.086

Table No.18. (Continued)

$u_{CE(1,1)}$	0.179	0.016	0.341
$u_{CE(1,2)}$	-0.179	-0.341	-0.016
$u_{CE(2,1)}$	-0.179	-0.341	-0.016
$u_{CE(2,2)}$	0.179	0.016	0.341
$u_{DE(1,1)}$	-0.014	-0.176	0.149
$u_{DE(1,2)}$	0.014	-0.149	0.176
$u_{DE(2,1)}$	0.014	-0.149	0.176
$u_{DE(2,2)}$	-0.014	-0.176	0.149
$u_{ABC(1,1,1)}$	0.180	-0.087	0.447
$u_{ABC(1,1,2)}$	-0.180	-0.447	0.087
$u_{ABC(1,2,1)}$	-0.287	-0.616	0.042
$u_{ABC(1,2,2)}$	0.287	-0.042	0.616
$u_{ABC(1,3,1)}$	0.107	-0.177	0.390
$u_{ABC(1,3,2)}$	-0.107	-0.390	0.177
$u_{ABC(2,1,1)}$	-0.300	-0.665	0.064
$u_{ABC(2,1,2)}$	0.300	-0.064	0.665
$u_{ABC(2,2,1)}$	0.051	-0.336	0.438
$u_{ABC(2,2,2)}$	-0.051	-0.438	0.336
$u_{ABC(2,3,1)}$	0.249	-0.067	0.565
$u_{ABC(3,3,2)}$	-0.249	-0.565	0.067
$u_{ABC(3,1,1)}$	0.120	-0.168	0.408
$u_{ABC(3,1,2)}$	-0.120	-0.408	0.168
$u_{ABC(3,2,1)}$	0.236	-0.115	0.586
$u_{ABC(3,2,2)}$	-0.236	-0.586	0.115
$u_{ABC(3,3,1)}$	-0.356	-0.673	-0.038
$u_{ABC(3,3,2)}$	0.356	0.038	0.673

Table No.18. (Continued)

$u_{ABD(1,1,1)}$	-0.128	-0.395	0.139
$u_{ABD(1,1,2)}$	0.128	-0.139	0.395
$u_{ABD(1,2,1)}$	0.132	-0.197	0.461
$u_{ABD(1,2,2)}$	-0.132	-0.461	0.197
$u_{ABD(1,3,1)}$	-0.004	-0.288	0.279
$u_{ABD(1,3,2)}$	0.004	-0.279	0.288
$u_{ABD(2,1,1)}$	0.371	0.006	0.735
$u_{ABD(2,1,2)}$	-0.371	-0.735	-0.006
$u_{ABD(2,2,1)}$	-0.368	-0.755	0.018
$u_{ABD(2,2,2)}$	0.368	-0.018	0.755
$u_{ABD(2,3,1)}$	-0.002	-0.318	0.314
$u_{ABD(2,3,2)}$	0.002	-0.314	0.318
$u_{ABD(3,1,1)}$	-0.243	-0.531	0.045
$u_{ABD(3,1,2)}$	0.243	-0.045	0.531
$u_{ABD(3,2,1)}$	0.236	-0.114	0.587
$u_{ABD(3,2,2)}$	-0.236	-0.587	0.114
$u_{ABD(3,3,1)}$	0.007	-0.311	0.324
$u_{ABD(3,3,2)}$	-0.007	-0.324	0.311
$u_{ABE(1,1,1)}$	0.023	-0.243	0.290
$u_{ABE(1,1,2)}$	-0.023	-0.290	0.243
$u_{ABE(1,2,1)}$	0.171	-0.158	0.500
$u_{ABE(1,2,2)}$	-0.171	-0.500	0.158
$u_{ABE(1,3,1)}$	-0.195	-0.478	0.089
$u_{ABE(1,3,2)}$	0.195	-0.089	0.478
$u_{ABE(2,1,1)}$	-0.117	-0.482	0.248
$u_{ABE(2,1,2)}$	0.117	-0.248	0.482

Table No.18. (Continued)

$u_{ABE(2,2,1)}$	-0.173	-0.560	0.213
$u_{ABE(2,2,2)}$	0.173	-0.213	0.560
$u_{ABE(2,3,1)}$	0.290	-0.026	0.606
$u_{ABE(2,3,2)}$	-0.290	-0.606	0.026
$u_{ABE(3,1,1)}$	0.094	-0.195	0.382
$u_{ABE(3,1,2)}$	-0.094	-0.382	0.195
$u_{ABE(3,2,1)}$	0.002	-0.348	0.353
$u_{ABE(3,2,2)}$	-0.002	-0.353	0.348
$u_{ABE(3,3,1)}$	-0.096	-0.413	0.222
$u_{ABE(3,3,2)}$	0.096	-0.222	0.413
$u_{BCE(1,1,1)}$	-0.527	-0.745	-0.308
$u_{BCE(1,1,2)}$	0.527	0.308	0.745
$u_{BCE(1,2,1)}$	0.527	0.308	0.745
$u_{BCE(1,2,2)}$	-0.527	-0.745	-0.308
$u_{BCE(2,1,1)}$	0.265	0.013	0.517
$u_{BCE(2,1,2)}$	-0.265	-0.517	-0.013
$u_{BCE(2,2,1)}$	-0.265	-0.517	-0.013
$u_{BCE(2,2,2)}$	0.265	0.013	0.517
$u_{BCE(3,1,1)}$	0.262	0.045	0.478
$u_{BCE(3,1,2)}$	-0.262	-0.478	-0.045
$u_{BCE(3,2,1)}$	-0.262	-0.478	-0.045
$u_{BCE(3,2,2)}$	0.262	0.045	0.478
$u_{BDE(1,1,1)}$	-0.026	-0.244	0.193
$u_{BDE(1,1,2)}$	0.026	-0.193	0.244
$u_{BDE(1,2,1)}$	0.026	-0.193	0.244
$u_{BDE(1,2,2)}$	-0.026	-0.244	0.193

Table No.18. (Continued)

$u_{BDE(2,1,1)}$	0.096	-0.156	0.348
$u_{BDE(2,1,2)}$	-0.096	-0.348	0.156
$u_{BDE(2,2,1)}$	-0.096	-0.348	0.156
$u_{BDE(2,2,2)}$	0.096	-0.156	0.348
$u_{BDE(3,1,1)}$	-0.070	-0.287	0.146
$u_{BDE(3,1,2)}$	0.070	-0.146	0.287
$u_{BDE(3,2,1)}$	0.070	-0.146	0.287
$u_{BDE(3,2,2)}$	-0.070	-0.287	0.146

Table 19. Estimate and 95% confidence limits of the parameters
(second order interaction effects)

u_{term}	Estimate of u	Lower 95% confidence limit of u	Upper 95% confidence limit of u
$u_{ABC(1,1,1)}$	0.180	-0.087	0.447
$u_{ABC(1,1,2)}$	-0.180	-0.447	0.087
$u_{ABC(1,2,1)}$	-0.287	-0.616	0.042
$u_{ABC(1,2,2)}$	0.287	-0.042	0.616
$u_{ABC(1,3,1)}$	0.107	-0.177	0.390
$u_{ABC(1,3,2)}$	-0.107	-0.390	0.177
$u_{ABC(2,1,1)}$	-0.300	-0.665	0.064
$u_{ABC(2,1,2)}$	0.300	-0.064	0.665
$u_{ABC(2,2,1)}$	0.051	-0.336	0.438
$u_{ABC(2,2,2)}$	-0.051	-0.438	0.336
$u_{ABC(2,3,1)}$	0.249	-0.067	0.565
$u_{ABC(3,3,2)}$	-0.249	-0.565	0.067
$u_{ABC(3,1,1)}$	0.120	-0.168	0.408
$u_{ABC(3,1,2)}$	-0.120	-0.408	0.168
$u_{ABC(3,2,1)}$	0.236	-0.115	0.586
$u_{ABC(3,2,2)}$	-0.236	-0.586	0.115
$u_{ABC(3,3,1)}$	-0.356	-0.673	-0.038
$u_{ABC(3,3,2)}$	0.356	0.038	0.673
$u_{ABD(1,1,1)}$	-0.128	-0.395	0.139
$u_{ABD(1,1,2)}$	0.128	-0.139	0.395
$u_{ABD(1,2,1)}$	0.132	-0.197	0.461
$u_{ABD(1,2,2)}$	-0.132	-0.461	0.197
$u_{ABD(1,3,1)}$	-0.004	-0.288	0.279

Table No.19. (Continued)

$u_{ABD(1,3,2)}$	0.004	-0.279	0.288
$u_{ABD(2,1,1)}$	0.371	0.006	0.735
$u_{ABD(2,1,2)}$	-0.371	-0.735	-0.006
$u_{ABD(2,2,1)}$	-0.368	-0.755	0.018
$u_{ABD(2,2,2)}$	0.368	-0.018	0.755
$u_{ABD(2,3,1)}$	-0.002	-0.318	0.314
$u_{ABD(2,3,2)}$	0.002	-0.314	0.318
$u_{ABD(3,1,1)}$	-0.243	-0.531	0.045
$u_{ABD(3,1,2)}$	0.243	-0.045	0.531
$u_{ABD(3,2,1)}$	0.236	-0.114	0.587
$u_{ABD(3,2,2)}$	-0.236	-0.587	0.114
$u_{ABD(3,3,1)}$	0.007	-0.311	0.324
$u_{ABD(3,3,2)}$	-0.007	-0.324	0.311
$u_{ABE(1,1,1)}$	0.023	-0.243	0.290
$u_{ABE(1,1,2)}$	-0.023	-0.290	0.243
$u_{ABE(1,2,1)}$	0.171	-0.158	0.500
$u_{ABE(1,2,2)}$	-0.171	-0.500	0.158
$u_{ABE(1,3,1)}$	-0.195	-0.478	0.089
$u_{ABE(1,3,2)}$	0.195	-0.089	0.478
$u_{ABE(2,1,1)}$	-0.117	-0.482	0.248
$u_{ABE(2,1,2)}$	0.117	-0.248	0.482
$u_{ABE(2,2,1)}$	-0.173	-0.560	0.213
$u_{ABE(2,2,2)}$	0.173	-0.213	0.560
$u_{ABE(2,3,1)}$	0.290	-0.026	0.606
$u_{ABE(2,3,2)}$	-0.290	-0.606	0.026
$u_{ABE(3,1,1)}$	0.094	-0.195	0.382

Table No.19. (Continued)

$u_{ABE(3,1,2)}$	-0.094	-0.382	0.195
$u_{ABE(3,2,1)}$	0.002	-0.348	0.353
$u_{ABE(3,2,2)}$	-0.002	-0.353	0.348
$u_{ABE(3,3,1)}$	-0.096	-0.413	0.222
$u_{ABE(3,3,2)}$	0.096	-0.222	0.413
$u_{BCE(1,1,1)}$	-0.527	-0.745	-0.308
$u_{BCE(1,1,2)}$	0.527	0.308	0.745
$u_{BCE(1,2,1)}$	0.527	0.308	0.745
$u_{BCE(1,2,2)}$	-0.527	-0.745	-0.308
$u_{BCE(2,1,1)}$	0.265	0.013	0.517
$u_{BCE(2,1,2)}$	-0.265	-0.517	-0.013
$u_{BCE(2,2,1)}$	-0.265	-0.517	-0.013
$u_{BCE(2,2,2)}$	0.265	0.013	0.517
$u_{BCE(3,1,1)}$	0.262	0.045	0.478
$u_{BCE(3,1,2)}$	-0.262	-0.478	-0.045
$u_{BCE(3,2,1)}$	-0.262	-0.478	-0.045
$u_{BCE(3,2,2)}$	0.262	0.045	0.478
$u_{BDE(1,1,1)}$	-0.026	-0.244	0.193
$u_{BDE(1,1,2)}$	0.026	-0.193	0.244
$u_{BDE(1,2,1)}$	0.026	-0.193	0.244
$u_{BDE(1,2,2)}$	-0.026	-0.244	0.193
$u_{BDE(2,1,1)}$	0.096	-0.156	0.348
$u_{BDE(2,1,2)}$	-0.096	-0.348	0.156
$u_{BDE(2,2,1)}$	-0.096	-0.348	0.156
$u_{BDE(2,2,2)}$	0.096	-0.156	0.348

Table No.19. (Continued)

$u_{BDE(3,1,1)}$	-0.070	-0.287	0.146
$u_{BDE(3,1,2)}$	0.070	-0.146	0.287
$u_{BDE(3,2,1)}$	0.070	-0.146	0.287
$u_{BDE(3,2,2)}$	-0.070	-0.287	0.146

REFERENCES

Adnett, N., & Slack, K. (2007). Are there economic incentives for non-traditional students to enter HE? The labour market as a barrier to widening participation. *Higher Education Quarterly, 61*(1), 23–36.

Ainley, P. (1994). *Degrees of difference*. London: Cassell.

Ainley, P. (1998). Higher education in a right state: Professionalising the proletariat or proletarianising the professions? In D. Jary & M. Parker (Eds.), *The new higher education: Issues and directions for the post-dearing University*. Staffordshire: Staffordshire University Press.

Ainley, P. (1999). *Learning policy, towards the certified society*. London: Macmillan.

Ainley, P. (2000). *Further than what? The place of FE under the learning and skills council*. Paper presented at the British Educational Research conference, Cardiff University, September 7–10. Retrieved January 12, 2006, from http://www.leeds.ac.uk/educol/documents/00001530.htm

Anderson, G., & Arsenault, N. (1998). *Fundamentals of educational research*. London: RoutledgeFalmer.

Archer, L. (2001). *Detours, dead-ends and blocked roads: Inner-city, working-class adults access to higher education*. Paper presented at SCUTREA, 3–5 July, University of East London. Retrieved January 12, 2006, from http://www.leeds.ac.uk/educol/documents/00002428.htm

Archer, L., Hutchings, M, & Ross, A. (2003). *Higher education and social class. Issues of exclusion and inclusion*. London: RoutledgeFalmer.

Argyris, C., & Schon, D. (1996). *Organisational learning II. Theory, method and practice*. London: Kogan Page.

Armstrong, P. (2000). *Include me out: Critique and contradiction in thinking about social exclusion and lifelong learning*. Paper presented at SCUTREA 3–5 July 2000. Retrieved January 12, 2006, from http://www.leeds.ac.uk/educol/documents/00001431.htm

Ashcroft, K. (1999). *The place of educational departments within the University*. Paper presented at the British Educational Research Association annual conference, University of Sussex at Brighton, September 2–5. Retrieved January 12, 2006, from http://www.leeds.ac.uk/educol/documents/00000 1085.htm

Ashworth, P., & Greasley, K. (2009). The phenomenology of 'approach to studying': The idiographic turn. *Studies in Higher Education, 34*(5), 561–576.

Atkinson, P., & Hammersley, M. (1995). *Ethnography: Principles in practice*. London: Routledge.

Baker, A. (1978). *English to get on with. Practice in phrasal/prepositional verbs*. London: Heinemann.

Baker, M. (2004). *OFFA opens its doors to controversy BBC News UK Education*. Retrieved January 12, 2006, from http://news.bbc.co.uk/2/hi/ik-news/education/4007247.stm

Ball, C. (1990). *More means different*. London: Royal Society of Arts.

Ball, S. J. (1994). *Politics and policy making in education: Explorations in policy sociology*. London: Routledge.

Ballantyne, R., Bain, J., & Parker, J. (1999). *Reflecting on University teaching, academics stories*. Canberra: Australian Government Publishing.

Ballard, B., & Clanchy, J. (1988). Literacy in the University: An 'Anthropological' Approach'. In G. Taylor, B. Ballard, V. Beasley, & D. Barton (Eds.), *Literacy: An introduction to the ecology of written communication*. Oxford: Blackwell.

Bandura, A. (1997). *Self-efficacy: The exercise of control*. New York: Freeman.

Barkas, L. A. (2000). *Changing further education. A search for meaning and survival in an unstable state*. Unpublished M.Phil thesis, University of York.

Barkas, L.A. (2008). Widening Participation and student literacy: the complex and contested role of student support centres. Unpublished PhD thesis, Institute of Education, University of London.

Barkas, L. A., & Bannon, R. (2002). *A guide to the dissemination of key skills*. Unpublished Internal report for Teesside University.

REFERENCES

Barkas, L. A., Bannon, R., & Hewitt, J. (2002). *Navigating the sea of skills.* Paper presented at 3rd annual skills conference, Skills Development in Higher Education: Forging Links. University of Hertfordshire, Hertfordshire Integrated Learning Projects.

Barnett, R. (1990). *The idea of higher education.* Buckingham: SRHE and Open University Press.

Barnett, R. (1994). *The limits of competence: Knowledge, higher education and society.* Buckingham: SRHE and Open University Press.

Barnett, R. (1997). *Higher education: A critical business.* Buckingham: SRHE and Open University Press.

Barnett, R. (1998). In or for the learning society. *Higher Education Quarterly, 52*(1), 7–21.

Barton, D. (1994). *Literacy: An introduction to the ecology of written language.* London: Blackwell.

Barton D., & Hamilton, M. (1998). *Local literacies: Reading and writing in one community.* London: Routledge.

Barton, D., Hamilton, M., & Ivanic, R. (Eds.). (2000). *Situated literacies. Reading and writing in contex.* London: Routledge.

Basic Skills Agency. (2006). Retrieved December 5, 2006, from http://www.basic-skills.co.uk/site/page. php?cms=0

Bates, I. (1997). *The competence and outcomes movement: The landscape of research, 1986–1996.* Retrieved December 5, 2006, from http://www.leeds.ac.uk/educol/documents/000022216.htm

Bathmaker, A. M. (2007). The impact of Skills for Life on adult basic skills in England: How should we interpret trends in participation and achievement? *International Journal of Lifelong Education, 26*(3), 295–313.

Bathmaker, A. M., & Avis S. J. (2007). How do I cope with that? The challenge of schooling cultures in further education for trainee FE lecturers. *British Educational Research Journal, 33*(4), 509–532.

Bathmaker, A. M., Brooks, G., Parry, G., & Smith D. (2007). *Dual-Sector further and higher education: Policies, organisations and students in transition.* Paper presented at the annual conference of the Society for Research in to Higher Education, Brighton, 11–13 December, 2007. Retrieved June 10, 2008, from http://www.shef.ac.uk/furtherhigher/papers.html

Bathmaker, A. M., & Thomas, W. (2009). Positioning themselves: An exploration of the nature and meaning of transitions in the context of dual sector FE/HE institutions in England. *Journal of Further and Higher Education, 33*(2), 119–130.

Baudrillard, J. (1983). *Simulations.* New York: Semiotexte.

Bauman, Z. (2001). *Community: Seeking safety in an insecure world.* Oxford: Polity.

Baynham, M. (1995). *Literacy practices: Investigating literacy in social contexts.* London: Longman.

Baynham, M. (2000). Academic writing in new and emergent areas. In M. R. Lea & B. Stierer (Eds.), *Student writing in higher education: New contexts.* Buckingham: SRHE and Open University Press.

Bazerman, C. (1988). *Shaping written knowledge: The genre and activity of the experimental article in science.* Madison, WI: University of Wisconsin Press.

Becher, T. (1989). *Academic tribes and territories: Intellectual enquiry and the cultures of disciplines.* Milton Keynes: SRHE and Open University Press.

Becher, T., & Trowler, P. R. (2001). *Academic tribes and territories* (2nd ed.). Buckingham: SRHE and Open University Press.

Beck. J. and M. F. D. Young. (2005). *The assault on the professions and the restructuring of academic and professional identities: a Bernsteinian analysis.* British Journal of Sociology of Education. 26, no.2: 183–197.

Beck, U. (1992). *Risk society: Towards a new modernity.* London: Sage.

Beck, U., Giddens, A., & Lash, S. (1994). *Reflexive modernization.* London: Polity.

Becker, G. (1992). *Human capital: A theoretical and empirical analysis with special reference to education.* Chicago: The University of Chicago Press.

Bell, J. (1996). *Graduateness: Some early thoughts.* Paper presented on 'Standards' as part of the Giving Credit Network at the University of Leeds on 29 October. Retrieved December 10, 2006, from http://www.leeds.ac.uk/educol/documents/000000068.htm

Bell, R., & Tight, M. (1993). *Open Universities: A British tradition.* Buckingham: SRHE and Open University Press.

Bennett, N., E. Dunne and B. Carre. (2000). *Skills Development in Higher Education and Employment.* Buckingham: The Society for Research into Higher Education and the Open University.

Bernstein, B. (1970). Education cannot compensate for society. *New Society, 26,* 344–347.

Bernstein, B. (1977). *Class, codes and control* (Vol. 3). London: Routledge & Kegan Paul.

Bernstein, B. (2000). *Pedagogy, symbolic control and identity.* London: Taylor & Francis.

Besnier. (1995). Literacy, emotion and authority: Reading and writing on a Polynesian atoll. In *Studies in the social and cultural foundations of language* (Vol. 17). Cambridge: Cambridge University Press.

Biggs, J. B. (1987). *Student approaches to learning and studying.* Melbourne: Australian Council for Educational Research.

Biggs, J. B. (1999). *Teaching for quality learning at University.* Buckingham: SRHE and Open University Press.

Biggs, J. B., & Collis, K. (1982). *Evaluating the quality of learning: The solo taxonomy.* New York: Academic Press.

Biglan, A. (1972). The characteristics of subject matter in different academic areas. *Journal of Applied Psychology, 57*(3), 195–203.

Birch, M. W. (1963). Maximum likelihood in three-way contingency tables. *Journal of the Royal Statistical Society, B*(25), 220–233.

BIS/Department for Business Innovation and Skills. (2009). *Skills for growth. The National skills strategy: Analytical paper.* Retrieved February 3, 2010, from http://www.bis.gov.uk/assets/biscore/corporate/docs/s/09-1468-skills-strategy-analytical-paper.pdf

Bishop, Y. M, Fienberg, S. E., & Holland, P. W. (1975). *Discrete multivariate analysis: Theory and practice.* Cambridge, MA: MIT Press.

Bligh, D. (1990). *Higher education.* London: Cassell Educational.

Blythman, M., & Orr, S. (2002). A joined-up approach to student support. In M. Peelo & T. Wareham (Eds.), *Failing students in higher education.* Buckingham: SRHE & Open University Press.

Blunkett, D. (1998). *The learning age, a renaissance for a new Britain.* Retrieved January 25, 2004, from http://www.leeds.ac.uk/educol/documents/000000654.htm

Bock, H. K. (1988). Academic literacy: Starting point or goal? In G. Taylor, B. Ballard, V. Beasley, H. Bock, J.Clanchy, & P. Nightingale (Eds.), *Literacy by degrees.* Milton Keynes: SRHE & Open University Press.

Bogdan, R. C., & Biklen, S. K. (1982). *Qualitative research for education: An introduction to theory and methods.* Massachusetts: Allyn & Bacon.

Booth, A. (1997). Listening to students; experiences and expectations in the transition to a history degree. *Studies in Higher Education, 22*(2), 205–220.

Boud, D. R., Cohen, R., & Walker, D. (Eds.). (1998). *Using experience for learning.* Buckingham: SRHE & Open University Press.

Boud, D. R., & Soloman, N. (2001). *Work-based learning: A new higher education?* Buckingham: Open University Press.

Boughey, C. (2002). Naming students' problems: An analysis of language-related discourses at a South African University. *Teaching in Higher Education, 7*(3), 295–307.

Bowden, J., & Marton F. (2004). *The University of learning. Beyond quality and competence.* London: RoutledgeFalmer.

Bowl, M. (2001). Experiencing the barriers: Non-traditional students entering higher education. *Research Papers in Education, 16*(2), 141–160.

Brannen, J. (1992). Combining qualitative and quantitative approaches: An overview. In Brannen (Ed.), *Qualitative and Quantitative Research.* Hants: Ashgate Publishing.

Brink, C. (2009). Standards will drop and other fears about the equality Agenda in higher education. *Higher Education Management and Policy, 21*(1), 19–37.

British Educational Research Association. (2004). *Revised ethical guidelines for educational research.* Retrieved September 1, 2005, from http://www.bera.ac.uk/publications/pdfs/ETHICA1.PDF

British Sociological Association Code of Ethics. (1973). Retrieved September 1, 2005, from http://www.britsoc.co.uk/new_site/index.php

REFERENCES

Brown, G., Bull, J., & Pendlebury M. (1997). *Assessing student learning in higher education.* London: Routledge.

Brown, M. B. (1976). Screening effects in multidimensional contingency tables. *Applied Statistics,* (25), 37–46.

Brown, P., & Scase, R. (1994). *Higher education & corporate realities. Class, culture and the decline of graduate careers.* London: UCL.

Brown, P., Green, A., & Lauder, H. (2001). *Globalization, competitiveness, and skill formation.* Oxford: Oxford University Press.

Brown, P., Hesketh, A., & Williams, S. (2004). *The mismanagement of talent. Employability and jobs in the knowledge economy.* Oxford: Oxford University Press.

Brown, P., Lauder, H., & Ashton, D. (2008). Education, globalisation and the future of the knowledge economy. *European Educational Research Journal, 7*(2), 131–156.

Bryman, A. (1992). Quantitative and qualitative research: Further reflections on their integration. In J. Brannen (Ed.), *Mixing methods: Qualitative and quantitative research.* Hants: Ashgate Publishing.

Burgess, R. G. (1985). The whole truth? Some ethical problems of research in a comprehensive school. In R. G. Burgess (Ed.), *Field methods in the study of education,* London: Falmer Press.

Burgess, R. G. (1993). Contractors and customers: A research relationship? In R. G. Burgess (Ed.), *Educational research & evaluation for policy & practice?* London: Falmer.

Burke, P. (2002). *Accessing education: Effectively widening participation.* Stoke-on-Trent: Trentham Books.

Cantril, H., Ames, A., Hastorf, A., & Illelson, W. (1949). Psychology and scientific research, III. The transactional view in psychological research. *Science,* 110, 517–522.

Carpentier, V. (2006). Funding in higher education and economic growth in France and the United Kingdom, 1921–2003. *Higher Education Management and Policy,* 18(3), 19–30.

Chown, M. (2007). *The Never-Ending days of being dead. Dispatches from the front line of science.* London: Faber and Faber.

Coates, G., & Adnett, N. (2002). *Encouraging cream-skimming and dreg-siphoning? Increasing competition between English HEIs.* Paper presented at the European conference on Educational Research, University of Lisbon, 11–14 September. Retrieved December 5, 2006, from http://www.leeds.ac.uk/educol/documents/00002369.htm

Coffield, F. (1998). 'A tale of three little pigs: Building the learning society with straw. *Evaluation and Research in Education,* 12(1), 44–58.

Coffield, F. (Ed.). (2000). *Differing visions of a learning society. Research findings* (Vols. 1 and 2). Bristol: Policy Press.

Coffield F., & Vignoles, A. (1997). Widening participation in higher education by ethnic minorities, women and alternative students. Report 5:1–19. In *The National Committee of Inquiry into Higher Education, (Dearing Report).* Norwich: HMSO.

Coffield, F., & Williamson, B. (1997). *The repositioning of higher education.* Buckingham: Open University Press.

Cohen, L., & Manion, L. (1994). *Research methods in education* (4th ed.). London: Routledge.

Cohen, M. (1993). *Listening to students' voices; What University students tell us about how they can learn.* Paper presented to annual meeting of the American Research Association, Atlanta, GA. Retrieved January 10, 1995, from http://www.aera.net/meetings/Default.aspx?menu_id=22&id=284

Commission on Social Justice, (CSJ). (1994). *Social justice: Strategies for national renewal.* London: Vintage.

Crawford, M., & Chaffin, R. (1986). The reader's construction of meaning: Cognitive research on gender and comprehension. In E. A. Flynn & P. P. Schweickart (Eds.), *Gender and reading: Essays on readers, texts, and contexts.* Baltimore: Johns Hopkins.

Creme, P., & Lea, M. (1997). *Writing at University: A guide for students.* Buckingham: Open University Press.

Crowther, J. (2000). *Participation and inclusion: Opening up a discourse of diminishing returns.* Paper presented at SCUTREA, 3–5 July, University of Nottingham. Retrieved September 5, 2006, from http://www.leeds.ac.uk/educol/documents/00001439.htm

Crowther, J. (2004). *What does lifelong learning do to the discourse of participation?* Paper presented at SCUTREA, 6–8 July, 2004, University of Sheffield. Retrieved September 5, 2006, from http://www. leeds.ac.uk/educol/documents/00003585.htm

Culler, J. (1983). *On deconstruction: Theory and criticism after structuralism.* London: Routledge.

D'Andrea, V., & Gosling, D. (2005). *Improving teaching and learning in higher education. A whole institution approach.* Maidenhead: Open University Press & McGraw-Hill.

Data Protection Act. (1998). Chapter 29. Crown copyright. Retrieved January 10, 2005, from http://www. opsi.gov.uk/acts/acts1998/19980029.htm

Davies, P., Williams, J., & Webb, S. (1997). Access to higher education in the late twentieth century: Policy, power and discourse. In J. Williams (Ed.), *Negotiating access to higher education. The discourse of selectivity and equity.* Buckingham: SRHE & Open University Press.

Davis, M. (1999). *Ethics and the University.* London: Routledge.

Dearing, R. (1996). *Dearing review on 16–19 education.* Retrieved January 10, 2005, from http://www. royalsoc.ac.uk/document.asp?tip=0&id=1899

Dearing, R. (1997). *National Committee of enquiry into higher education.* London: HMSO.

Denzin, N. (1970). Strategies of multiple triangulation. In N. Denzin (Ed.), *The research act in sociology: A theoretical introduction to sociological method.* New York: McGraw-Hill.

Denzin, N. K., & Lincoln Y. S. (2000). Introduction: The discipline and practice of qualitative research. In N. K. Denzin & Y. S. Lincoln (Eds.), *Handbook of qualitative research* (2nd ed.). London: Sage.

Department for Education and Skills and Department of Employment. (1991). London: HMSO.

DfES. (2002). *Widening participation in higher education.* Retrieved January 10, 2005, from http://www. dfes.gov.uk/hegateway/uploads/EWParticipation.pdf

Department for Education and Employmnet. (2001). *Skills for life. The national strategy for improving adult literacy and numeracy skills.* Nottingham: DfEE.

DfES/QCA. (2002). *Pathways to proficiency. The alignment of language proficiency scales for assessing competence in English Language.* Nottingham: DfES.

DfES. (2003). *The future of higher education.* London: HMSO.

DfES. (2006). Retrieved January 20, 2006, from http://www.dfes.gov.uk/hegateway/hereform/index.cfm

Department for Innovation, Universities and Skills (DIUS). (2007). Retrieved September 1, 2007, from http://www.dius.gov.uk/

Derrida, J. (1976). *Of grammatology.* Translated from the French by Gayatri Chakravorty Spivak. Baltimore: Johns Hopkins University Press.

Devlin, M. (2002). Taking responsibility for learning isn't everything: A case for developing tertiary students' conceptions of learning. *Teaching in Higher Education, 7*(2), 125–138.

Dewey, J. (1916). *Democracy and Education.* New York: Macmillan.

Dewey, J. (1938). *Experience and Education.* New York: Macmillan.

Donnelly, R. (2006). Exploring lecturers' self-perception of change in teaching practice. *Teaching in Higher Education, 11*(2), 203–217.

Doyle, M. (2003). *Discourses of employability and empowerment: Foundation degrees and 'third Way' discursive repertoires.* Retrieved January 10, 2005, from http://www.leeds.ac.uk/educol/documents/ 00002421.htm

Drew, S. (2001). Student perceptions of what helps them learn and develop in higher education. *Teaching in Higher Education, 6*(3), 309–329.

Duke, C. (1992). *The learning university. Towards a new paradigm?* Buckingham: SRHE & Open University Press.

Duke, C. (2002). *Managing the learning university.* Buckingham: SRHE and Open University Press.

Duncan, G (2008, September 16) *Lehman Brothers collapse sends shockwave round world.* Retrieved January 14, 2004 from: http://business.timesonline.co.uk/tol/business/industry_sectors/banking_and_ finance/article4761892.ece

Dunne, E. (Ed.). (1999). *The learning society. International perspectives on core skills in higher education.* London: Kogan Page.

REFERENCES

Durkin, K., & Main, A. (2002). Discipline-based study skills support for first-year undergraduate students. *Active Learning in Higher Education, 3*(1), 24–39.

Earwaker, J. (1992). *Helping and supporting student.* Buckingham: SRHE and Open University Press.

Education and Training for the 21st Century. Retrieved January 28, 2005, from http://www.bopcris. ac.uk/bopall/ref23241.html

Education Reform Act. (1988). Retrieved January 28, 2005, from http://www.legislation.hmso.gov.uk/ acts/acts1988/Ukpga_19880040_en_1.htm.

Edwards, R., & Nicoll, K. (2001). Researching the rhetoric of lifelong learning. *Journal of Education Policy, 16*(2), 103–112.

Edwards, R., Miller, N., Small, N., & Tait, A. (Eds.). (2002). *Supporting lifelong learning. making policy work* (Vol. 3). London: RoutledgeFalmer.

Elliot, D., & Stern, J. E. (Eds.). (1997). *Research ehtics. A reader.* Hanover, NH: University of New England Press.

Elliott, G. (1999). *Lifelong learning. The politics of the new learning environment.* London: Higher Education Policy Studies Series 44 and Jessica Kingsley.

Elliott, G. (2004). *Regionalism in higher education in England: The politics of collaboration and competition.* Paper presented at the British Educational Research Association Annual Conference, University of Manchester, 16–18 September, 2004. Retrieved January 28, 2005, from http://www.leeds. ac.uk/educol/documents/00002241.htm

Ellis, C., & Bochner, A. P. (2000). Autoethnography, personal narrative, reflexivity: Researcher as subject. In N. K. Denzin & Y. S. Lincoln (Eds.), *Handbook of Qualitative Research* (2nd ed.). London: Sage.

Entwistle, N. (2000, November). *Promoting deep learning trough teaching and assessment: Conceptual frameworks and educational contexts.* Paper presented at the Teaching and Learning Research Project annual conference, Leicester. Retrieved January 28, 2005, from http://www.leeds.ac.uk/educol/ documents/00002401.htm

Entwistle, N. J., & Marton, F. (1994). Knowledge objects: Understandings constituted through intensive academic study. *British Journal of Educational Psychology, 64,* 61–78.

Entiwistle, N. J., & Tair, H. (1995). Approaches to studying and perceptions of the learning environment across the disciplines. In N. Hativa & M. Marincovich (Eds.), *Disciplinary differences in teaching and learning: Implications for practice.* San Francisco: Jossey-Bass.

Evans, K., Brown, A., & Oates, T. (1987). *Developing Work-based learning: An evaluative review of the YTS core skills project.* Guildford: University of Surrey and Manpower Services Commission.

Everitt, B. S. (1977). *The analysis of contingency tables.* London: Chapman and Hall.

Fairburn, G. J., & Winch, C. (1996). *Reading, writing and reasoning: A guide for students* (2nd ed.). Buckingham: Open University Press.

Fairclough, N. (1989). *Language and power.* London: Longman.

Fairclough, N. (1992). *Discourse and social change.* Cambridge: Polity Press.

Fairclough, N. (1995). *Critical discourse analysis.* London: Longman.

Fairclough, N. (2000a). *New labour, new language?* London: Routledge.

Fairclough, N. (2000b). Multiliteracies and language: Orders of discourse and intertextuality. In B. Cope & M. Kalantzis (Eds.), *Multiliteracies. Literacy learning and the design of social futures.* London: Routledge.

Fazey, D. M. A., & Fazey, J. A. (2001). The potential for autonomy in learning; perceptions of competence, motivation and locus of control in first year undergraduate studies. *Studies in Higher Education, 26*(3), 345–361.

Ferguson, R. (1990). Introduction: Invisible centre. In R. Ferguson (Ed.), *Out there: Marginalization and contemporary cultures* (pp. 9–14). New York and Cambridge: New Museum of Contemporary Art and MIT.

Fichter, J. H., & Kolb, W. L. (1954). Ethical limitations on sociological reporting. In J. H. Fichter (Ed.), *Social relations in the Urban Parish.* Chicago: University of Chicago Press.

Field, J. (1999). *Skills and employability in the limelight: Exploring official discourses of training'*. Paper presented at SCUTREA, 5–7 July, 1999, University of Warwick. Retrieved January 28, 2005, from http://www.leeds.ac.uk/educol/documents/000000991.htm

Field, J. (2002). *Lifelong learning and the new educational order*. London: Trentham.

Fienberg, S. E. (1980). *The analysis of cross-classified categorical data* (2nd ed.). Cambridge, MA: MIT Press.

Foucault, M. (1972). *The archaeology of knowledge*. Translated from the French by A. M. Sheridan Smith. London: Tavistock.

Foucault, M. (1977). *Discipline and punish: The birth of the prison*. London: Penguin.

Foucault, M. (1980). *Power/Knowledge: Selected interviews and other writings, 1972–1977*. Translated from the French by C. Gordon. New York: Pantheon.

Friere, P. (1973). *Pedagogy of the oppressed*. New York: Seabury.

Fryer, S. (1997). *Learning for the twenty first century*. London: National Advisory Group for Continuing Education and Lifelong Learning [NAGCELL] and DfEE.

Fryer, S. (1999). *Creating learning cultures – next steps in achieving the learning age*. (NAGCELL) London: DfEE.

Fuller, A., & Unwin, L. (2001). Context and meaning in apprenticeship: The changing relationship between apprentices, employers and communities in England. In *SKOPE Monograph* (Vol. 3). Universities of Oxford and Warwick.

Fund for the Development of Teaching. (2008). Retrieved from http://www.heacademy.ac.uk/ourwork/networks/fdtl

Further and Higher Education Act. (1992). Retrieved February 12, 2006, from http://www.opsi.gov.uk/ACTS/acts1992/Ukpga_19920013_en_1.htm

Future of Higher Education (The). (2003). White paper. Retrieved January 31, 2005, from http://www.dfes.gov.uk/hegateway/strategy/hestrategy/

Future of Higher Education Act. (2004). Retrieved February 20, 2006, from http://www.opsi.gov.uk/ACTS/en2004/2004en08.htm

Gallie, D. (1994). Patterns of skill change: Upskilling, deskilling or polarisation? In R. Penn, M. Rose, & J. Rubery (Eds.), *Skill and occupational change*. Oxford: Oxford University Press.

Gamache, P. (2002). University students as creators of personal knowledge: an alternative epistemological view. *Teaching in Higher Education, 7*(3), 277–293.

Ganobcsik-Williams, L. (Ed.). (2006). *Teaching academic writing in UK higher education*. Basingstoke: Palgrave Macmillan.

Garrison, D. R., Cleveland-Innes, M., & Fung, T. (2004). Student role adjustment in online communities of inquiry: Model and instrument validation. *Journal of Asynchronous Learning Networks, 8*(2), 128–135. Retrieved February 20, 2006, from http://www.sloan-c.org/publications/jaln/v8n2/pdf/v8n2_garrison.pdf

Gee, J. P. (1990). *Social linguistics and literacies: Ideology in discourses*. Basingstoke: Falmer Press.

Gee, J. P. (1996). *Social linguistics and literacies: Selected essays*. London: Falmer.

Gee, J. P. (2000). The new literacy studies: From socially situated to the work of the social. In D. Barton, M. Hamilton, & R. Ivanic (Eds.), *Situated literacies. Reading and writing in context*. London: Routledge.

Gee, J. P., & Lankshear, C. (1995). The new work order: Critical language awareness and fast capitalism. *Texts in Discourses in the Cultural Politics of Education, 16*(1), 5–19.

Geertz, C. (1975). *The interpretation of cultures: Selected essays*. London: Falmer Press.

Geertz, C. (1983). *Local knowledge. Further essays in interpretive anthropology*. New York: HarperCollins.

Gibbs, G. (1981). *Teaching students to Learn – A student centred approach*. Buckingham: SRHE and Open University Press.

Gibbs, G. (1992). Improving quality of student learning through course design. In R. Barnett (Ed.), *Learning to effect*. Buckingham: SRHE and Open University Press.

Gibbs, G. (2000). Are the pedagogies of the disciplines really different? In D. Rust (Ed.), *Improving student learning through the disciplines*. Oxford: Oxford Centre for Staff and Learning Development.

Gibbs, P. (2001). Higher education as a market: A problem or solution? *Studies in Higher Education, 26*(1), 85–94.

REFERENCES

Giddens, A. (1998). *The third way. The renewal of social democracy.* Cambridge: Polity Press.

Giddens, A. and Turner, J. (1987). *Social Theory Today.* Cambridge. Polity Press.

Gittens, R. (1993). *An introduction to literacy teaching.* London: The Adult Literacy and Basic Skills Unit.

Glaser, B., & Strauss, A. (1967). *The discovery of grounded theory.* Chicago: Aldine.

Glennerster, H. (2002). United Kingdom 1997–2001. *Oxford Review of Economic Policy, 18*(2), 120–136.

Goffman, E. (1981). *Forms of talk.* Oxford: Blackwell.

Goodman, L. A. (1970). The multivariate analysis of qualitative data: Interactions among multiple classifications. *Journal of the American Statistical Association, 65,* 226–256.

Green, A. (1997). *Education, globalisation and the nation state.* London: Macmillan.

Griffin, C. (1999). Lifelong learning and welfare reform. *International Journal of Lifelong Education,* 18(6), 431–452.

Guba, E. G., & Lincoln, Y. S. (1989). Competing paradigms in qualitative research. In N. K. Denzin, & Y. S. Lincoln (Eds.), *The landscape of qualitative research. Theories and issues.* London: Sage.

Hager, P., & Hodkinson, A. (2009). Moving beyond the metaphor of transfer of learning. *British Educational Research Journal, 35*(4), 619–638.

Haggis, T. (2001). *Whose learning story? Differing pictures of 'adult' learners in higher education.* Paper presented at SCUTREA 3–5 July. Retrieved January 28, 2005, from http://www.leeds.ac.uk/educol/documents/00002466.htm

Haggis, T. (2003). *Theorising learning in higher education: Epistemology, metaphor, and complexity.* Paper presented at the British Educational Research Association annual conference, Heriot-Watt University, Edinburgh, 11–13 September. Retrieved January 28, 2005, from http://www.leeds.ac.uk/educol/documents/00002456.htm

Haggis, T. (2006). Pedagogies for diversity: Retaining critical challenge amidst fears of dumbing down. *Studies in Higher Education, 31*(5), 521–535.

Haggis, T. (2009). What have we been thinking of? A critical overview of 40 years of student learning research in higher education. *Studies in Higher Education, 34*(4), 377–390.

Haggis, T., & Pouget, M. (2002). Trying to be motivated: Perspectives on learning from younger students accessing higher education. *Teaching in Higher Education, 7*(3), 323–336.

Halliday, M. A. K. (1978). *Language as social semiotic: The social interpretation of language and meaning.* London: Francis Pinter.

Halliday, M. A. K. (1994). *Introduction to functional grammar* (2nd ed.). London: Edward Arnold.

Halliday, M. A. K., & Hasan, R. (1989). *Language, context and text: Aspects of language in a social-semiotic perspective* (2nd ed.). Oxford: Oxford University Press.

Halliday, M. A. K., & Martin, J. (1993). *Writing science.* London: Falmer Press.

Halsey, A. H. (Ed.). (1992). Opening wide the doors of higher education. In *National commission of education briefings.* London: Heineman for Paul Hamlyn Foundation.

Halsey, A. H. (1995). *Decline of Donnish Dominion.* Oxford: Clarendon Press.

Hammersley, M. (1992). Deconstructing the qualitative-quantitative divide. In J. Brannen (Ed.), *Mixing methods: Qualitative and quantitative research.* Aldershot: Ashgate Publishing.

Hammersley, M. (1993). On the teacher as researcher. In M. Hammersley (Ed.), *Educational research: Current issues.* London: Paul Chapman.

Hammersley, M. (2000). The sky is never blue for modernisers: The threat posed by David Blunkett's offer of partnership to social science. *Research Intelligence, 72,* 12–13.

Hammersley, M. (2002). *Educational research. Policymaking and practice.* London: Paul Chapman.

Hammilton, M. (1994). Introduction: Signposts. In M. Hammilton, D. Barton, & R. Ivanic (Eds.), *Worlds of literacy.* Clevedon: Multilingual Matters.

Hammilton, M., Barton, D., & Ivanic, R. (Eds.). (1994). *Worlds of literacy.* Clevedon: Multilingual Matters.

Hare, P. (2000). *Constraints and incentives in the UK University system.* Heriott-Watt University, School of Management, Economics Division, Discussion Paper No: 2000/3.

Harris, R. (2007, September 13). Proper English is not a luxury. Letter in the *Times Higher Education Supplement,* 15.

Hawking, S. (1988). *A Brief History of Time.* London, Bantam Dell.

Harvey, L. (2002). Evaluation for what? *Teaching in Higher Education, 7*(3), 245–263.

Harvey, L., & Knight, P. (1996). *Transforming higher education*. Buckingham: Open University Press.

Hayashi, C. (1950). On the quantification of qualitative data from the mathematico-statistical point of view. *Annals of the Institute of Statistical Mathematics, 2*(1), 35–47.

Hayashi, C. (1952). On the prediction of phenomena from qualitative data and the quantification of qualitative data from the mathematico-statistical point of view. *Annals of the Institute of Statistical Mathematics, 3*(2), 69–98.

Hayes, J. (1997). Access to higher education: An exploration of realities and possibilities. *International Journal of Inclusive Education, 1*(3), 257–265.

Henkel, M. (2000). *Academic identities and policy change in higher education*. London: Jessica Kingsley.

Higgins, R. (2000). *Be more critical! Rethinking assessment feedback*. Paper presented at the British Educational Research Association conference, Cardiff University, September 7–10. Retrieved January 28, 2005, http://www.leeds.ac.uk/educol/documents/00001548.htm

Higher Education Academy (The). (2008). Retrieved January 20, 2008, from http://www.heacademy.ac.uk/

Higher Education Funding Council For England. (2001). *Strategies for learning and teaching in higher education*. 01/37, Bristol: HEFCE.

Higher Education Funding Council For England. (2004). *Regional profiles of higher education*. Retrieved February 2, 2005, from C:\DocumentsandSettings\u0004918\LocalSettings\TemporaryInternetFiles\OLK6\Regional profiles of Higher Education 2004.doc

Higher Education Role Analysis. (2005). Retrieved January 20, 2006, from http://hera.ucea.ac.uk/

Higher Education Statistics Agency. (2007). Retrieved September 1, 2007, from http://www.nao.org.uk/

Higher Education Quality Committee. (1996). Retrieved February 2, 2005, from http://www.che.ac.za/heqc/heqc.php

Hirst, P. (1974). *Knowledge and the curriculum*. London: Routledge and Kegan Paul.

Hoadley-Maidment, E. (2000). From personal experience to reflective practitioner: Academic literacies and professional education. In M. R. Lea & B. Stierer (Eds.), *Student writing in higher education: New contexts*. Buckingham: SRHE and Open University Press.

Hodgson, A. & Spours, K. (Eds.). (1997). *Dearing and beyond, 14–19 qualifications, frameworks and systems*. London: Kogan Page.

Hounsell, D. (1987). Essay writing and the quality of feedback. In J. Richardson, M. W. Eysenck & D. W. Piper (Eds.), *Student learning: Research in education and cognitive psychology*. Milton Keynes: Open University Press.

House of Commons. (2001). *Select committee publications*. Retrieved February 21, 2005, from http://www.publications.parliament.uk/pa/ld/ldselect.htm

Huddleston, P., & Unwin, L. (2002). *Teaching and learning in further education* (2nd ed.). London: Routledge.

Hunt, C. (2007). Diversity and pedagogic practice: Reflections on the role of an adult educator in higher education. *Teaching in Higher Education, 12*(5–6), 765–779.

Hyland, K. (2004). *Disciplinary Discourses. Social Interactions in Academic Writing*. Michigan: University of Michigan Press.

Hyland, T. (1996). Access and credit and the learning society. *Journal of Access Studies, 11*(2), 153–164.

Hyland, T. (1998). Morality and further education; towards a critical values foundation for the post-compulsory sector in Britain. *Journal of Moral Education, 27*(3), 333–344.

Hyland, T, & Johnson, S. (1998). Of cabbages and key skills. *Journal of Educational Studies, 46*(2), 163–172.

Hyland, T. (2003). Learning, work and community. Vocational studies and social values in the learning age. In J. Field, & M. Leicester (Eds.), *Lifelong learning. Education across the lifespan*. London: RoutledgeFalmer.

Ivanic, R. (1997). *Writing and identity. The discoursal construction of identity in academic writing*. Philadelphia: John Benjamins.

REFERENCES

Ivanic, R., Clark, R., & Rimmershaw R. (2000). 'What am I supposed to Make of This? The messages conveyed to students by tutors' comments. In M. R. Lea & B. Stierer (Eds.), *Student writing in higher education: New contexts*. Buckingham: SRHE and Open University Press.

Ivanic, R., & Lea, M. R. (2006). 'New contexts, new challenges: The teaching of writing in UK higher education. In L. Ganobcsik-Williams (Ed.), *Teaching academic writing in UK higher education*. Basingstoke: Palgrave MacMillan.

Jessup, G. (1990). *Accreditation of prior learning in the context of national vocational qualifications: A summary of the national programme*. London: NCVQ.

Johnston, R., (1999). *High way, My way, No way, third way – locating social purpose learning in a risk society?* Paper presented at SCUTREA, 5–7 July, University of Warwick. Retrieved December 5, 2006, from http://www.leeds.ac.uk/educol/documents/000001003.htm

Kafka, F. (1963). *The trial* (Willa & E. Muir, Trans.). London: Secker & Warburg.

Kember, D. (1997). A re-conceptualisation of the research into University Academics' conceptions of teaching. *Learning and Instruction, 7*(3), 255–275.

Kember, D. (2001). Beliefs about knowledge and the process of teaching and learning as a factor in adjusting to study in Higher Education. *Studies in Higher Education, 26*, 205–221.

Kennedy, H. (1997). *Learning works: Widening participation in further education*. Coventry: FEFC.

Kenny, J. D. (2009). Managing a modern university: Is it time for a rethink? *Higher Education Research & Development, 28*(6), 629–642.

Ketteridge, S., Marshall, S., & Fry, H. (Eds.). (2002). *The effective academic: A handbook for enhanced academic practice*. London: Kogan Page.

Kitwood, T. M. (1977). Values in adolescent life: Towards a critical description. Unpublished PhD thesis, University of Bradford, School of Research in Education.

Knight, P. (1996). Independent study, independent studies and 'core skills' in higher education. In J. Tait & P. Knight (Eds.), *The management of independent learning*. London: Kogan Page in association with SEDA.

Knight, P. (2001). Complexity and curriculum: A process approach to curriculum making. *Teaching in Higher Education, 6*(3), 369–380.

Knight, P., & York, M. (2003). *Assessment, learning and employability*. Buckingham: SRHE and Open University Press.

Kogan, M. & Kogan, D. (1983). *The attack on higher education*. London: Kogan Page.

Kolb, D. A. (1984). *Experiential learning experience as the source of learning and development*. New Jersey: Prentice Hall.

Kreber, C. (2003). The relationship between students' course perception and their approaches to studying in undergraduate science courses. A Canadian experience. *Higher Education Research & Development, 11*(1), 57–75.

Kreber C., & Cranton, P. A. (2000). Exploring the scholarship of teaching. *Journal of Higher Education, 71*, 476–495.

Kress, G. R., & Van Leeuwen, T. (2006). *Reading images: The grammar of visual design*. London: Routledge.

Krugman, P. (1996). Making sense of the competiveness debate. *Oxford Review of Economic Policy, 12*(3), 17–25.

Lankshear, C. (1997). *Changing literacies*. Buckingham: Open University Press.

Lather, P. (1986). Research as praxis. *Harvard Educational Review, 56*, 257–277.

Lather, P. (1991). *Getting smart. Feminist research and pedagogy with/in the postmodern*. London: Routledge.

Lather, P. (1992). Critical frames in educational research: Feminist and post-structural perspectives. *Theory into Practice, 31*(2), 1–13.

Lather, P. (1993). Fertile obsession: Validity after post-structuralism, *Sociological Quarterly, 35*, 673–694.

Latour, B. (1987). *Science in action: How to follow scientists and engineers through society*. Cambridge, MA: Harvard University Press.

Lauder, H., & Mehralizader, Y. (2001). Globalization, multinationals, and the labour market. In P. Brown, A. Green, & H. Lauder (Eds.), *Globalization, competitiveness, and skill formation*. Oxford: Oxford University Press.

Laurillard, D. (2002). *Rethinking University teaching. A framework for the effective use of learning technologies* (2nd ed.). London: Routledge Falmer.

Lea, M. R., & Street, B. (2000). Student writing and staff feedback in higher education. An academic literacies approach. In M. R. Lea & B. Stierer (Eds.), *Student writing in higher education. New contexts*. Buckingham: SRHE and Open University Press.

Lea, M. R., & Stierer, B. (Eds.). (2000). *Student writing in higher education. New contexts*. Buckingham: SRHE and Open University Press.

Leadbeater, C. (1999). *Living on thin air: The new Economy*. London: Viking.

Learning Age [The]. (1998). Retrieved January 31, 2005, from http://www.lifelonglearning.co.uk/green paper/

Learning and Skills Council. (2005). Retrieved January 31, 2005, from http://www.lsc.gov.uk/National/default.htm

Learning and Skills Council. (2007). Retrieved September 1, 2007, from http://www.lsc.gov.uk/

Leavis, F. R. (1965). *The common pursuit*. London: Chatto and Windus.

Leitch, S. (2006). *Review of skills, prosperity for all in the global economy – world class skills*. Retrieved November 1, 2009, from http://www.hm-treasury.gov.uk/leitch_review_index.htm

Light, G., & Cox, R. (2001). *Learning & teaching in higher education. The reflective professional*. London: Sage.

Lillis, T. M. (2006). Moving towards an academic literacies pedagogy: Dialogues of participation. In L. Ganobcsik-Williams (Ed.), *Teaching academic writing in UK higher education*. Basingstoke: Palgrave Macmillan.

Lillis, T. M., & Turner, J. (2001). Student writing in H.E: Contemporary confusion, traditional concerns. *Teaching in Higher Education, 6*(1), 57–68.

Lincoln, Y. S., & Guba, E. G. (1985). *Naturalistic inquiry*. Beverly Hills, CA: Sage.

Literacy Task Force. (1997). *A reading revolution: How we can teach every child to read well*. London: Literacy Task Force.

Long, P., & Trickler, T. (2004). *Do first year undergraduates find what they expect?* Paper presented at the British Educational Research Association annual conference, University of Manchester, 16–18 September, 2004. Retrieved January 28, 2006, from http://www.leeds.ac.uk/educol/documents/0000 3696.htm

Longden, B. (2002) Retention rates – renewed interest but whose interest is being served? *Research Papers in Education*. 17(1), 3-30.

Lowe, H., & Cook, A. (2003). Mind the gap: Are students prepared for higher education? *Journal of Further and Higher Education, 27*(1), 53–76.

Lucas, N. (2004). The FENTO Fandango: National standards, compulsory teaching qualifications and the growing regulation of FE college teachers. *Journal of Further and Higher Education, 28*(1), 35–51.

Lum, G. (2004). On the Non-discursive nature of competence. *Educational Philosophy and Theory, 36*(5), 485–496.

Lyotard, J. F. (1984). *The postmodern condition: A report on knowledge*. Manchester: Manchester University.

Malcolm, J., & Zukas, M. (2002). *Altered states of teacher identity: The impact of scrutiny and regulation on pedagogic thinking and practice*. SCUTREA, 2–4 July 2002, University of Stirling. Retrieved January 28, 2005, from http://www.leeds.ac.uk/educol/documents/00002085.htm

Marks, A., Turner, E., & Osbourne, M. (2003). Not for the likes of me: The overlapping effect of social class and gender factors in the decision made by adults not to participate in higher education. *Journal of Further and Higher Education, 27*(4), 347–364.

Marton, F., & Saljo, R. (1976). On qualitative differences in learning- outcome and process. *British Journal of Educational Psychology, 46*, 4–11.

REFERENCES

Marton, F., & Ramsden, P. (1986). Do learning skills courses improve student learning? In J. Bowden (Ed.), *Student learning; research into practice*. Melbourne: University of Melbourne.

Marton, F., & Booth, S. A. (1997). *Learning and awareness*. Hillsdale, NJ: Lawrence Erlbaum.

Marton, F., Hounsell, D., & Entwistle, N. (Eds.) (1997). *The experience of learning: Implications for teaching and studying in higher education* (2nd ed.). Edinburgh: Scottish Academic Press.

Maslow, A. (1973). *The farther reaches of human nature*. Harmondsworth: Penguin.

Massey, A., & Walford, G. (Eds.) (1999). Methodological triangulation, or how to get lost without being found out. Explorations in methodology. *Studies in Educational Ethnography, 2*, 183–197.

McCormack, P. (2003). *Fortress education: A study of widening participation in an elite UK University*. PhD Thesis, Newcastle University No. 201 29648X. British Library: DX 228961.

McCormick, K. (1994). *The culture of reading and the teaching of English*. Manchester: Manchester University Press.

McCullagh, P., & Nelder, J. A. (1989). *Generalized linear models* (2nd ed.). London: Chapman and Hall.

McInnis, C. (2001). *Signs of disengagement? The changing undergraduate experience in Australian universities*. Melbourne: Centre for the Study of Higher Education, University of Melbourne. Retrieved July 25, 2002, from http://www.cshe.unimelb.edu.au/downloads/InaugLec23-8-01.pdf

McNair, S. (1997). *Getting the most out of HE: Supporting learner autonomy*. Sheffield: DfEE.

Medway, P. (2005). Literacy and the idea of English. *Changing English, 12*(1), 9–29.

Meek, V. (2000). Diversity and marketisation of higher education: Incompatible concepts? *Higher Education Policy, 13*, 23–49.

Merriam, S. B. (1988). *Case study research in education. A qualitative approach*. London: Jossey-Bass.

Meyer, J., & Shannon, M. (2001). A triangulated approach to the modelling of learning outcomes in first year economics. *Higher Education Research & Development, 20*, 127–145.

Mills, M. (2007, September, 13). Universities torn between two masters. *The Times Higher Education Supplement*, 15.

Mitchell, C. (1984). Case studies. In R. Ellen (Ed.), *Ethnography: A guide to general conduct*. London: Academic Press.

Moser, C. (1999). *A fresh start - improving literacy and numeracy*. DfEE Ref: CMBS 1. Retrieved January 28, 2005, from http://www.literacytrust.org.uk/socialinclusion/adults/moser.html

Monroe, J. (Ed.). (2002). *Writing and revising the disciplines*. New York: Cornell University Press.

Myers, G. (1990). *Writing Biology*. Madison, WI: University of Wisconsin Press.

National Audit Office. (2006) and (2007). Retrieved September 12, 2007, from http://www.nao.org.uk/

National Skills Targets. (2002). *The learning and skills council*. Retrieved December 5, 2006, from http://www.lsc.gov.uk/National/Media/PressReleases/Archive/LSC+sets+new+ambitious+learning+and+skills+targets+for+the+nation.htm

National Student Survey. (2005). Retrieved December 5, 2006, from http://www.thestudentsurvey.com/

Neuman, R. (2001). Disciplinary differences and University teaching. *Studies in Higher Education, 26*(2), 135–146.

Newman, M. (2010, March 18) Teaching and research escape 9% grant cuts. Retrieved March 18, 2010 from: http://www.timeshighereducation.co.uk/story.asp?storycode=410879

Newman, S., & K. Jahdi. (2009). Marketisation of education: Marketing, rhetoric and reality. *Journal of Further and Higher Education, 33*(1), 1–11.

Nicoll, K. (2002). *Lifelong learning: The altering of state policy*. Paper presented at SCUTREA, 2–4 July 2002, University of Stirling. Retrieved January 28, 2005, from http://www.leeds.ac.uk/educol/documents/00002089.htm

Nightingale, P. (1988). Language and learning: A bibliographical essay. In G. Taylor, B. Ballard, V. Beasley, H. Bock, J. Clanchy, & P. Nightingale. *Literacy by degrees*. Milton Keynes: SRHE and Open University Press.

Nixon, J. (1996). Professional identity and the restructuring of higher education. *Studies in Higher Education, 21*(1), 5–16.

Nixon. J. (2003). Professional renewal as a condition of institutional change. *International Studies in the Sociology of Education, 13*(1), 3–15.

134

Norton, L. S., Tilley, A. J., Newstead, S. E., Franklyn-Stokes, A., (2001). The pressures of assessment in undergraduate courses and their effect on student behaviours. *Assessment and Evaluation in Higher Education, 26*(3), 269–284.

Pardoe, S. (2000). A question of attribution: The indeterminacy of learning form experience. In M. L. Lea & B. Stierer. (Eds.), *Student writing in higher education. New contexts.* Buckingham: SRHE & O.U. Press.

Parry, G. (1995). England, Wales and Northern Ireland. In P. Davies (Ed.), *Adults in higher education. International perspectives on access and participation.* London: Jessica Kingsley.

Parry, G. (2005). British Higher Education and the prism of devolution. In T. Tapper & D. Palfreyman (Eds.), *Understanding mass higher education. Comparative persepectives on access.* Abingdon: RoutledgeFalmer.

Parry, G. (2009). Higher Education, further education and the English experiment. *Higher Education Quarterly, 63*(4), 322–342.

Parry, G., Davies, P., & Williams, J. (2004). *Difference, diversity and distinctiveness. Higher Education in the learning skills sector.* London: Learning and Skills Development Agency.

Pearson, K. (1900). Mathematical contributions to the theory of evolution in the inheritance of characters not capable of exact quantitative measurement, VIII. *Philosophical Translations Royal Society London Series, A*(195), 79–150.

Peelo, M. (1994). *Helping students with study problems.* Buckingham: SRHE and Open University Press.

Peterson, A. D. C. (1971). *A hundred years of education.* London: Gerald Duckworth.

Pollitt, C., & Boukaert, G. (2002). *Public management reform: A comparative analysis.* Oxford: Oxford University Press.

Powell, R., Smith, R., & Reakes, A., (2003). *Basic skills and key skills: A review of international literature.* NFER. Retrieved January 28, 2005, from http://www.leeds.ac.uk/educol/documents/00003620.htm

Powley, F. (2001). *Lifelong learning or lifelong yearning: An analysis of widening participation policy implementation in Cumbria.* PhD. Thesis, Lancaster. British Library Number: 51090358 DX 228968.

Preece, J. (1999). *Combatting social exclusion in university adult education.* Aldershot: Ashgate.

Preece, S., & Godfrey, J. (2009). *Academic literacy practices and widening participation: First year undergraduates on an academic writing programme.* Retrieved November 1, 2009, from http://www.wmin.ac.uk

Pring, R., & Hayward, G. (2006). *Review of 14–19 education and training.* Retrieved September 1, 2007, from http://www.nuffield14-19review.org.uk/

Prosser, M., & Trigwell, K. (1999). *Understanding learning and teaching.* Buckingham: Open University Press.

Prosser, M., Ramsden, P, Trigwell K., & Martin, E. (2003). Dissonance in experience of teaching and its relation to the quality of student learning. *Studies in Higher Education, 28*(1), 38–48.

Purcell, K., Wilton, N., & Elias, P. (2003). *Older and wiser? Age and experience in the graduate labour market. Researching graduate careers seven years on.* A project jointly funded by the Economic and Social Research Council and the Higher Education Careers Services Unit, Employment Studies Research Unit, Warwick Institute for Employment Research.

Purcell, K., Wilton, N., & Elias, P. (2007). Hard lessons for lifelong learners? Age and experience in the Graduate labour market. *Higher Education Quarterly, 61*(1), 57–82.

Qualifications and Curriculum Authority. (2006). Retrieved September 2, 2006, from http://www.qca.org.uk/

Ramsden, P. (Ed.). (1988). *Improving learning: New perspectives.* London: Kogan Page.

Ramsden, P. (1998). *Learning to lead in higher education.* London: Routledge.

Ramsden, P. (1999). *Teaching for quality learning at University.* Buckingham: SRHE and Open University Press.

Ranson, S. (Ed.). (1998). *Inside the learning society.* London: Cassell.

Raudenbush, S. W., & Bryk, A. S. (2002). *Hierarchical linear models: Applications and data analysis methods.* London: Sage.

REFERENCES

Reynolds, S. (2003). *Should there be a new language of widening participation?* Paper presented at SCUTREA 1–3 July, University of Wales. Retrieved January 28, 2005, from http://www.leeds.ac. uk/educol/documents/00003118.htm

Richardson, J. (1997). Dispelling some myths about mature students in higher education: Study skills, approaches to studying, and intellectual ability. In P. Sutherland (Ed.), *Adult learning: A reader.* London: HMSO.

Richardson, L. (2000). Writing: A method of inquiry. In N. K. Denzin & Y. Lincoln (Eds.), *Collecting and interpreting qualitative materials.* London: Sage.

Rikowski, G. (2001, March 24). *Six points on education for human capital, employers' needs and business in new labour's green paper.* Paper prepared for an open meeting on Promoting Comprehensive Education in the 21st Century, London. Retrieved January 28, 2005, from http://www.leeds.ac.uk/ educol/documents/00001708.htm

Robbins, L. R., Lord. (1963). *Higher Education: Report of the committee appointed by the Prime Minister under the Chairmanship of Lord Robbins.* London: HMSO.

Robbins, L. R., Lord. (1980). *Higher Education revisited.* London: Macmillan.

Robinson, J. (1997). *The myth of parity of esteem. Earnings and qualifications.* A Discussion Paper No. 34. London: Centre for Economic Performance.

Rogers, C. R. (1945). The non-directive method as a technique for social research. *American Journal of Sociology, 50*(3), 279–283.

Rogers, C. R. (1969). *The freedom to learn.* Columbus, OH: Merrill.

Rolfe, H. (2002). Students' demands and expectations in an age of reduced financial support: The perspectives of lecturers in four English Universities. *Journal of Higher Education Policy and Management,* 24(2), 171–182.

Rose, R. (2001). *The impact of social capital on health.* Glasgow: Centre for the Study of Public Policy.

Rowland, S. (2003). Academic development: A practical or a theoretical business? In H. Eggins & R. Macdonald (Eds.), *The scholarship of academic development.* Buckingham: SRHE & Open University Press.

Royal College of Psychiatrists. (2006). *The mental health of students in higher education.* (Council Report CR112 January, 2003). London: Royal College of Psychiatrists.

Russell Group of Universities. (2005). Retrieved January 31, 2005, from http://www.russellgroup.ac. uk/about.html

Sandel, M. (2009). *Reith Lectures. A New Citizenship.* Retrieved July 25, 2010 from: http://downloads.bbc. co.uk/rmhttp/radio4/transcripts/20090609 thereithlecturesmarketsandmorals.rtf

Savin-Baden, M. (2000). *Problem-based learning in higher education: Untold stories.* Buckingham: Open University Press.

Schon, D. A. (1987). *Educating the reflective practitioner.* San Francisco: Jossey-Bass.

Scott, P. (Ed.). (1998). *The globalization of higher education.* Buckingham: SRHE and Open University Press.

Sheffield Hallam University. (2002). *TLTP3 key to key skills project report.* Retrieved July 3, 2002, from http://www.shu.ac.uk/keytokey

Shephard, J. (2006, February 10). Tutors despair at illiterate freshers. *The Times Higher Education Supplement,* 1. Retrieved February 14, 2007, from http://www.timeshighereducation.co.uk/story.asp? storyCode=201255&sectioncode=26

Shrek (2001). Retrieved July 3, 2002, from http://www.imdb.com/title/tt0126029/combined

Silver, H., & Silver, P. (1997). *Students, changing roles, changing lives.* Buckingham: SRHE and Open University Press.

Skelton, A. (2004). Understanding 'teaching excellence' in higher education: A critical evaluation of the National teaching fellowship scheme. *Studies in Higher Education, 29*(4), 451–468.

Slee, R. (2001). Social justice and the changing directions in educational research: The case of inclusive education. *International Journal of Inclusive Education, 5*(2), 167–177.

Smith, H, Armstrong, M., & Brown, S. (1999). *Benchmarking and threshold standards in higher education.* London: Kogan Page.

Spiro, M. E. (1996). Postmodernist anthropology, subjectivity and science. A modernist critique. *Comparative Studies in Society and History, V*, 759–780.

Stake, R. E. (1978). The case study method in social inquiry. *Educational Researcher, 7*(2), 5–8.

Stake, R. E. (1996). *The art of case study research*. Thousand Oaks, CA: Sage.

Stake, R. E. (2000). Case studies. In N. K. Denzin & Y. S. Lincoln (Eds.), *Handbook of qualitative research* (2nd ed.). London: Sage.

Standish, P. (2002). Disciplining the profession: Subjects subject to procedure. *Educational Philosophy and Theory, 34*(1), 5–23.

Startreck (2010) Retrieved July, 25, 2010 from: http://www.startrek.com/

Statistical Package for Social Sciences (SPSS). (2002 and 2004). *Versions 10 and 11*. Retrieved June 1, 2005 and November 1, 2007, from http://www.spss.com/

Steer, R., Edward, S., Hodgson, A., & Coffield, F. (2005). *A new learning and skills landscape? Is the post-compulsory education and training sector in England being transformed?* Paper presented at the European conference on Educational Research, University College Dublin, 7–10 September.

Stierer, B. (1997). *Mastering education: A preliminary analysis of academic literacy practices within master-level courses in education*. Milton Keynes: Open University.

Strauss, A. L., & Corbin, J. (1990). *Basics of qualitative research: Grounded theory procedures and techniques*. Newbury Park, CA: Sage.

Street, B. (1994). *Social literacies: Critical approaches to literacy in development, ethnography and education*. London: Longman.

Stronach, I., & Morris, B. (1994). Polemical notes on educational evaluation in the Age of policy Hysteria. *Evaluation and Research in Education, 8*(1), 5–19.

Stronach, I., & MacLure, M. (1997). *Educational research undone. The postmodern embrace*. Buckingham: Open University Press.

Sutton Trust. (2004). Annual report. Retrieved January 23, 2006, from http://www.suttontrust.com/reports/report04.pdf

Tait, A. (2000). Planning student support for open and distance learning. *Open Learning, 15*(3), 287–299.

Taylor, A. J. P. (1993). *The Troublemakers*. London, Pimlico.

Taylor, G. (1988). The literacy of knowing: Content and form in students' English. In G. Taylor, B. Ballard, V. Beasley, H. Bock, J. Clanchy, & P. Nightingale (Eds.), *Literacy by degrees*. Milton Keynes: SRHE and Open University Press.

Teaching Quality Information (TQi). (2006). HEFCE. Retrieved January 23, 2006, from http://www.hefce.ac.uk/Pubs/Circlets/2006/cl23_06/

Teelken, C., & Braaem, G. (2002). *Guarding and preserving the autonomy of the individual professional, controlling for potentially dysfunctional consequences of performance measurement in organisations in higher education*. Paper resented at the European conference on Educational Research, University of Lisbon 11–14 September, 2002. Retrieved January 23, 2006, from http://www.leeds.ac.uk/educol/documents/00003253.htm

Tett, l. (2004). *Learning and literacies: Telling stories and writing lives*. Paper presented at SCUTREA, 6–8 July, 2004, University of Sheffield. Retrieved January 25, 2006, from http://www.leeds.ac.uk/educol/documents/00003612.htm

Thomas, L., Cooper, M., & Quinne J. (Eds.). (2002). *Collaboration to widen participation in Higher Education*. Stoke-on-Trent: Trentham Books.

Thomas, L., Quinn, J., Slack, K., & Casey, L. (2003). *Effective approaches to retaining students in higher education. Directory of practice. The student services research project*. Staffordshire: Institute of Access Studies.

Thompson, J. (2000). Introduction. In J. Thompson (Ed.), *Stretching the academy. The politics and practice of widening participation in higher education*. Leicester: NIACE.

Tight, M. (1998). Education, education, education! The vision of lifelong learning in the Kennedy, dearing and fryer reports. *Oxford Review of Education, 24*(4), 473–485.

Timesonline. (2006). *Education*. Retrieved January 12, 2007, from http://www.timesonline.co.uk/tol/life_and_style/education/

REFERENCES

Tolle, E. (2005). *A new earth. Awakening to your life's purpose*. London: Michael Joseph.

Tomlinson, M. (2004). *14–19 curriuculum and qualifications reform*. Retrieved January 31, 2005, from www.14–19reform.gov.uk

Tomlinson, S. (2001). *Education in a post-welfare society*. Buckingham: Open University Press.

Tuckman, B. W. (1972). *Conducting educational research*. New York: Harcourt Brace Jovanovich.

UCAS. (2005). The universities central organisation that processes applications for full-time undergraduate courses at UK universities and colleges. Retrieved February 1, 2005, from http://www.ucas.com/

University For Industry (Ufl). (2005). Retrieved January 25, 2005, from http://www.ufi.com/home/default.asp

University League Tables. (2006). Retrieved December 5, 2006, from Times online: http://www.times online.co.uk/section/0,,716,00.html#startcontent

Universities UK. (2010). Retrieved April 2, 2010, from http://www.universitiesuk.ac.uk

Unwin, L. (1993). Training credits: The pilot doomed to succeed. In W. Richardson, D. Finegold, & J. Woodhouse (Eds.), *The reform of post-16 education and training in England and Wales*. Harlow: Longman.

Unwin, L. (1997). Reforming the work-based route: Problems and potential for change. In A. Hodgson & K. Spours (Eds.), *Dearing and beyond, 14–19 qualifications, frameworks and system*. London: Kogan Page.

Unwin, L. (2004a). Twenty-first century vocational education in the United Kingdom: What would Dickens think? *Pedagogy, Culture and Society, 12*(2), 175–199.

Unwin, L. (2004b). Growing beans with Thoreau: Rescuing skills and vocational education from the UK's deficit approach. *Oxford Review of Education, 30*(1), 147–160.

Unwin, L. (2009). *Sensuality, sustainability and social justice. Vocational education in changing times*. London: Institute of Education.

Uuwin, L., & Wellington, J. (2001). *Young people's perspectives on education, training and employment: Realizing their potential*. London: Kogan Page.

Upton, G. J. G. (1978). *The analysis of cross-tabulated data*. London: John Wiley.

Werhane, P., & Doering, J. (1997). Conflicts of interest and conflicts of commitment. In D. Elliot & J. E. Stern (Eds.), *Research ethics. A reader*. Hanover, NH: University of New England Press.

Whitty, G. (2002). *Making sense of education policy: Studies in the sociology and politics of education*. London: Paul Chapman.

Williams, J. (1997). Institutional rhetorics and realities. In J. Williams (Ed.). *Negotiating access to higher education. The discourse of selectivity and equity*. Buckingham: SRHE and Open University Press.

Williams, K and Carroll, J. (2009). Referencing and Understanding Plagiarism. London: Palgrave.

Wilson, A. L. (2009). Learning to read: Discourse analysis and the study and practice of adult education.

Wingate, U. (2006). Doing away with 'study skills'. *Teaching in Higher Education*, 11(4), 457–469 Studies in Continuing Education, 31(1), 1–12.

Wingate, U. (2007). A framework for transition: Supporting 'Learning to learn' in higher education. *Higher Education Quarterly, 61*(3), 391–405.

Winter, R. (2009). Academic manager or managed academic? Academic identity schisms in higher education. *Journal of Higher Education Policy and Management, 31*(2), 121–131.

Wolf, A. (2002). *Does education matter? Myths about education and economic growth*. London: Penguin.

Wolf, D. M., & Kolb, D. A. (1984). Career development, personal growth and experiential learning. In D. Kolb, I. Rubin, & J. MacIntre (Eds.), *Organisational psychology: Readings on human behaviour* (4th ed.). New Jersey: Prentice-Hall.

Woodhead, C. (1999, April 24). Millenium reputations. *The Daily Telegraph*, p. 1.

Woodrow, M., & Thomas, L. (2002). Pyramids or spiders? Cross-section collaboration to widen participation. Learning from international experiences. A comparative study to identify the most effective ways for post compulsory education institutions to work together to widen participation. In L. Thomas, M.Cooper, & J. Quinne (Eds.), *Collaboration to widen participation in higher education*. Stoke-on-Trent: Trentham Books.

Wright, D. B. (2002). *First steps in statistics*. London: Sage.

Yanagasawa, Y. (2002). *Using statistics and SPSS.* Course Handbook and Lecture Notes, University of Teesside.

Yelland, C. (2000). *Designing the SSC's writing skills Website.* Unpublished Internal Report for the University of Teesside.

Yin, R. K. (1994). *Case study research: Design and methods* (2nd ed.). California: Sage.

Yorke, M., & Longden, B. (2004). *Retention and student success in higher education.* Berkshire: SRHE.

Young, M. (1998). Post-compulsory education for a learning society. In S. Ranson (Ed.), *Inside the learning society.* London: Cassell.

Young, P. (2006). Out of balance: Lecturers' perceptions of differential status and rewards in relation to teaching and research. *Teaching in Higher Education, 11*(2), 191–202.

Young, M. (2009). Education, globalisation and the 'voice of knowledge'. *Journal of Education and Work, 22*(3), 193–204.

Young, M., & J. Muller. (2010). Three educational scenarios for the future: Lessons from the sociology of knowledge. *European Journal of Education, 45*(1), 11–27.

Yule, G. U. (1900). On the association of attributes in statistics: With illustration from the material of the childhood society. *Philosophical Translations Royal Society London Series, A*(194), 257–319.

Zimmerman, B. J. (1989). A social cognitive view of self-regulated academic learning. *Journal of Educational Psychology, 81*(3), 329–339.

CPSIA information can be obtained at www.ICGtesting.com
Printed in the USA
267880BV00004B/20/P